I'm going to have a little house

Engendering Latin America
Volume 4

Editors:

DONNA J. GUY
University of Arizona

MARY KARASCH
Oakland University

ASUNCIÓN LAVRIN
Arizona State University

I'm going to have a little house

The Second Diary of Carolina Maria de Jesus

(Casa de Alvenaria: Diário de uma ex-favelada)

CAROLINA MARIA DE JESUS

Translated by Melvin S. Arrington Jr. and Robert M. Levine
Afterword by Robert M. Levine

University of Nebraska Press
Lincoln and London

Originally published as *Casa de Alvenaria:
Diário de uma ex-favelada* (Rio de Janeiro:
Editora Paulo de Azevedo Ltda., 1961)

© Vera Eunice de Jesus Lima.
Translation © 1997 by the
University of Nebraska Press
All rights reserved
Manufactured in the United States
of America

☺ The paper in this book meets the mini-
mum requirements of American National
Standard for Information Sciences—
Permanence of Paper for Printed Library
Materials, ANSI z39.48-1984.

Library of Congress Cataloging-in-
Publication Data

Jesus, Carolina Maria de.
[Casa de alvenaria. English]
I'm going to have a little house: the second
diary of Carolina Maria de Jesus / translated by Melvin S. Arrington Jr. and
Robert M. Levine; afterword by Robert
M. Levine.
p.   cm.
(Engendering Latin America; v. 4)
ISBN 0-8032-2583-0 (cloth: alk. paper).
ISBN 0-8032-7599-4 (pbk.: alk. paper).
1. Jesus, Carolina Maria de—Diaries.
2. Blacks—Brazil—São Paulo—Social
   conditions.
3. Poor—Brazil—São Paulo—Social life
   and customs.
4. City and town life—Brazil—São Paulo.
5. São Paulo (Brazil)—Social conditions.
6. São Paulo (Brazil)—Social life and
   customs.
7. Poor—Brazil—São Paulo—Diaries.
8. Blacks—Brazil—São Paulo—Diaries.
I. Title.
II. Series.
F2651.S253J4713   1997
981'.6100496—dc21   96-53134
                              CIP

For
Peggy, Joey, and David
and
Terry, Linda, and Debra

contents

illustrations

Following page 94

preface

Carolina Maria de Jesus was a destitute black Brazilian woman, born in 1914 in the rural interior, who migrated to São Paulo, the largest industrial city in Latin America, seeking work and a better life. The great-grandchild of slaves, she became literate on her own, having attended school for less than two years. As a young girl she developed a passion for reading, which later fed her desire to write down her feelings and to tell her story. In 1958 a reporter, Audálio Dantas, discovered that she had written a diary about her hard life; he managed to edit it, publish some of the entries in his newspaper, and in August 1960, have it printed under the title *Quarto de Despejo* (Livraria Francisco Alves; *Child of the Dark,* New York: E. P. Dutton, 1962). It became the best-selling book in Brazilian history and made its author world famous. Carolina wrote four other books, which were published without success, and many poems, short stories, and memoir fragments. Only a few years after her mercurial success, however, she was forced back into poverty. She died in 1977 ignored.

This translation of Carolina's second published diary, *Casa de Alvenaria: Diário de uma ex-favelada* (Rio de Janeiro: Editora Paulo de Azevedo Ltda., 1961), emerged from an oral history project initiated in 1990 by Robert M. Levine and José Carlos Sebe Bom Meihy in order to learn about the lives of Carolina's children in the years following her death. The oral histories awakened interest in Carolina's fate and led to several new projects related to the life and work of the black Brazilian author. Levine and Sebe published *Cinderela Negra: A Saga de Carolina Maria de Jesus* (Rio de Janeiro: Editora UFRJ, 1995) and *The Life and Death of Carolina Maria de Jesus* (Albuquerque: University of New Mexico Press, 1995). Andrea Paula dos Santos, one of the students involved in the project, has written a book (to be published in 1997 by Editora Loyola in São Paulo) on the lower-class women in Guarujá (São Paulo state) who call themselves "Carolinas." Sebe and the literary scholar Marisa Lajolo published in 1996 a book about Carolina's poetry, *Antologia Pessoal* (Rio de Janeiro: UFRJ). A translation of Carolina's autobiographical *Diário de Bitita* is planned. Royalties from all of these books have been earmarked for Carolina's grandchildren. Finally, the U.S. Library of Congress office in Rio de Janeiro has worked out an arrangement with the Biblioteca Nacional to microfilm more than four thousand pages of Carolina's surviving archive, including unpublished essays, poems, and novels. The original project, then, has taken on a life of its own among readers of Carolina's works, inspired by her insight and by the story of her life.

I'm Going to Have a Little House plays a major part in the reconstruction of that story. Published in Brazil but soon forgotten, the second diary was also translated into Spanish and published in Argentina, but it has never before been translated into English. The entries span from 5 May 1960 to 21 May 1961.

This translation aims at capturing Carolina's awkward writing style, which Brazilians often criticized. For example, Carolina starts many sentences with "I thought:". She often uses full names—Sr. Antonio Soeiro Cabral—when in normal speech one would use only the first or last name, or she uses codes, calling Audálio Dantas "the reporter." She refers to her female peers as "Dona," a formal term akin to "Mrs." that always precedes the first name, and distinguishes between Mr. (Senhor), which usually she does not capitalize, and Dr., which she uses for people who appear to be educated. Sometimes, for no apparent reason, she adds emphasis to titles: *Dr.*, or *Dona*. She is very inconsistent in her use of accents, a mark of an unschooled person. Her phrasing is often unusual, a style she developed when she did not dream that her writing would be read by anyone except her children. She comments directly on what she did: "I looked at." She repeats certain phrases: "I awoke at," "I had the impression that." She writes about details that may not always be necessary: "I greeted [so-and-so] . . . I said goodbye and took my leave." She often reiterates themes such as the high cost of living for the poor and recurrently tells how people stopped her in the street after she became famous. She repeats words where more experienced authors would probably have substituted synonyms.

This is the way Carolina wrote, and we have to the best of our ability sought to capture it in translation. Although we have attempted to preserve her distinctive writing style, spellings of names and use of accent marks have been made consistent in the translation. *Sr.* is abbreviated consistently in the translation, although Carolina sometimes wrote it out. We have also followed Carolina's capitalization.

Carolina sometimes used "big" words, and some Brazilian critics have alleged that her editor must have inserted them for her. This is not true: Carolina did have an extensive vocabulary, and almost all of the time she used words correctly. Dantas did make long and extensive cuts from her notebooks, but he did not put words in her mouth.

Ellipses within parentheses, or (. . .), indicate where Dantas deleted material from her diary entries. Where the diary entries themselves included dots to indicate pauses, the translation uses ellipses without parentheses.

Sometimes Carolina tells us about people who were important to her but about whom nothing more is known three and a half decades after her diary's publication. For this reason many names, such as Father Comaru, physician Italo Fittipaldi, Mario Brasini, Mauricio Ferraz de Camargo, Dona Brasilia Pagani, Mestre Jou, reporter Heitor Augusto, and dozens of others unknown to us, are not further identified, although these individuals touched her life in significant ways.

A Note on Brazilian Currency

Carolina frequently tells how much things cost. Today, things would cost about five times as much: 1,000 cruzeiros (Cr$1,000) was worth about $5.30 in U.S. currency in 1960, the equivalent of $26.50 in 1996 dollars. Inflation eroded the value of the cruzeiro by 65 percent from 1960 to 1961. Many of the sums mentioned by Carolina may seem tiny to us today: Cr$200 ($1.00) for a cab fare; Cr$12 ($0.06) for bread; Cr$510 ($2.70) for a leg of pork; Cr$10 (less than

$0.01) for a newspaper; Cr$50,000 ($265) for a loan to open a workshop; Cr$400,000 ($1,272) to pay off the mortgage on a house. In 1960, however, the official monthly minimum wage was the equivalent of $216, but few wage earners in the lower class actually made this amount. Before she had her diary published, Carolina rarely earned more than a dollar a day.

I'm going to have a little house

May 5, 1960   I got up at 5 A.M. to get the kids' clothes ready so we could go to the bookstore. I'm not going to make coffee because I don't have any sugar or any money for bread. I picked up a bag and went looking for tin cans, glass, scrap iron, and any other metal I could find, took what I collected, and went to sell it. I haven't had time lately to sell to Sr. Manoel.[1] I made Cr$22.[2] I spent Cr$12 on bread. Sr. Luiz Barbosa, who lives near the favela, gave me some kindling. I told him that today I am going to sign a contract with Francisco Alves Press to publish my book. He told me he had seen my picture in newspapers and magazines and he gave me some more wood. When I went back I picked it up, put it in my bag, and carried everything back to the favela.

. . . José Carlos came in saying that he was hungry. We are going to get ready to go downtown. We will see if Vera's father left money with the judge. João returned from school in a good mood because I had given him some bread. We left. I passed by Sr. Eduardo's store and asked him if he would sell me some sandwiches for the children. He didn't have any bread. I'm the only one who noticed the sadness in my kids' eyes; that's because I'm a mother. We went downtown. We passed the Municipal Market. Vera was looking at the ground to see if she could find something to eat. She couldn't find anything. She started to cry and didn't want to go any further. I told her, "Let's go to the judge to collect the money and I'll buy something for you."

She hesitated. I slapped her. Then I felt bad about what I had done and thought, Poor things! They're hungry, and on top of that they get spanked. I kept on walking while she stayed behind. My boys were at the newsstand looking at [Caryl] Chessman's picture.[3]

When I turned around, Vera was gone. I went back to look for her and I entered the market shouting, "Vera! Vera! Vera!"

I asked one of the security guards if he had seen a little girl.

"No!"

A million thoughts went running through my head. My heart started pounding. I ran through the market and all around outside it. I saw a woman from the favela and asked her if she had seen my little girl.

"I haven't seen her."

"I'm on my way to the Francisco Alves Bookstore to sign a contract. They're going to publish my book."

The people who overheard me say I was going to sign a contract with Francisco Alves Press stopped and stared at me. I ran out of the market shouting, "Vera! Vera! Vera!"

My boys were looking for her also. A woman came up to me and asked if I was looking for a little girl.

"Yes! Have you seen her?"

"She was in my store."

I asked the woman her name.

"Antonieta."

"Oh, Dona Antonieta, thank you and may God give you a handsome boyfriend."

She smiled and with obvious pleasure responded, "I already have a boyfriend. I'm married and I love my husband very much."

I saw a whole bunch of people with Vera right in the middle of them. She was crying. When she saw me, she put on a happy face. I thanked the women in the store and asked them their names. I told them it was so I could include them in my diary and that I was on my way to the bookstore to sign a contract to have my book published. They said, "You don't have to do that."

I looked at the name of the store. Cantareira Fabrics. I heard a male voice say, "I'd like to get my store's name in the newspapers."

"You'll see it, God willing." I thanked everyone, told them I was in a hurry, and ran out. In the Praça da Sé cars were parading around carrying deformed children soliciting aid. My children looked at the deformed bodies. I said to a couple holding a little boy, "Do you see those children? Their parents must be sad. And

there are some parents that beat their kids for breaking a
neighbor's window or for playing in the mud or for saying curse
words. And what if the children couldn't speak at all?"
I bent down and said in the little boy's ear, "That's right, son.
You're going to break windows, play ball, run, and have a perfect
childhood."
He smiled.
I said goodbye and went on to the courthouse. I went to
get Vera's money. The money was there. That cheered me up. I
collected it, signed a receipt, and told the clerk that I was going to
sign a contract for my book and that tomorrow I would be in all
the newspapers. And that I had to write because Vera's father
doesn't help me.
I told the clerk goodbye and went to buy *kibes* [Middle Eastern
meat patties] for my kids. When they saw me with the package they
smiled. I gave each one of them a *kibe* and a pastry. They kept on
smiling while they ate. I looked at my watch. It was 4 P.M.
. . . We arrived at the Francisco Alves Bookstore. I asked for
Paulo Dantas [a writer who was one of the directors of the press].
The woman at the cash register phoned him. He saw me from
upstairs and told me to come up in the elevator. The bookstore is
a cheerful place. As I entered the elevator I noticed that it was old.
It must have been in service for sixty years. It gives the impression
that the bookstore is a relic of São Paulo. I really appreciate old
things.
Sr. Del Nero walked up to me and spoke. Sr. Lélio de Castro
Andrade [the managing director] also came forward and Paulo
Dantas introduced us. As we talked, I became less timid and I
began to feel like I was in heaven. My blackness was not an
obstacle. And my shabby clothes weren't a problem either.
Reporters began to arrive. They asked me questions, took my
picture, and read passages from my diary. Several journalists
and photographers were there. I asked, "What newspaper are
you with?"
"*Ultima Hora.*"
I read a section of the diary. I was getting weak because I had
gone without anything to eat. The reporter for *Ultima Hora* gave me

Cr$20. When I entered the bookstore and started talking to the cashier, a man gave me Cr$10—he thought I was a beggar. The cashier told me, "Take it!"

The people in the bookstore asked, "Who is she?"

"She's a writer and she lives in the favela."

"Oh!" they exclaimed.

Other reporters arrived. They interviewed me and spoke to Paulo Dantas. And they read parts of my diary. At 5:30 Audálio [Dantas, the reporter who helped Carolina to publish her diary] showed up with the television crew. He introduced me, I signed the contract, and they filmed me.

. . . Sr. Lélio de Castro Andrade gave the reporter Cr$2,000 to give to me. My kids were happy. I told João that tomorrow I would buy meat and make him a steak because he has been begging me for a long time to cook one for him. He was happy and smiling. I knew that he was thinking about a plate of rice with steak and onions.

In the past all children had on their minds was dancing to music. They were happy. Nowadays, all they think about is food.

. . . At 6 P.M. I said goodbye. Sr. Lélio gave me his card so that I could call on him. I mentioned the books I am working on.

Today I earned:

scrap metal	22 cruzeiros
bookstore customer	10
Ultima Hora reporter	20
Vera's father	500
Sr. Lélio	2,000
	2,552

I said goodbye to everybody in the bookstore and had my picture taken standing next to the store window. When we got to the trolley stop, I took the children to eat in a restaurant. They enjoyed it. (. . .) It was 8 P.M. when I entered Sr. Eduardo's store. I paid him Cr$260 that I had been owing him for a long time and I bought some cheese for Cr$180, a kilo of sugar, and coffee. I showed Sr. Eduardo the contract so that he could read it and I told him, "Tomorrow I'm going to be in all the newspapers."

I said goodbye to Sr. Eduardo, whose eyes were staring at my face as if he were seeing me for the first time.

João told me, "You're spending a lot."

"Our life of poverty is going to end," I said, smiling.

When I got back to the favela I was sleepy and happy. I looked up and let my eyes rest on my cross. I thought, I ought to pray.

João said, "Hey Mom, I'm going to tell you something."

"What is it?" I asked uneasily, thinking, I wonder if it's something serious?

"It's really great to eat until you get full."

Life was sad because we were hungry. But the change in our lives has been sublime.

Vera said, "Hooray for Audálio!"

"Hooray!"

"Should we tag Audálio?" [Apparently, Dantas was present.]

They tagged him and kept on yelling. We got ready and went to bed.

May 6 I got up at 4 A.M. I went to read the news about Chessman. (. . .) The whole world is condemning the United States because of Chessman's execution.

Clouds hid the sun and I felt cold. (. . .) I went shopping at the Japanese man's shop. I bought three kilos of rice, a kilo of black beans, three bars of soap, flour, garlic, and indigo dye. When I returned to the favela I went to fix lunch for the kids. The children came to tell me that they saw my photograph in the newspapers. Today I'm the sensation of the neighborhood. I made lunch: rice, beans, fried steak, and salad. João liked the meal and shouted out, "Long live Carolina!"

I smiled. He looked at me for a long time and said to me, "We've got food now and you don't have to cry."

They are happy because they have eaten.

May 7 I didn't go out to buy bread. My kids ate cheese. João has changed. He is calmer, always smiling. I don't know how many times I have told him, "João, you're like an animal!"

But now that we have food in the house, he has changed. He's no longer "João the Brute"—now he's "João the Gentleman." It's just that hunger makes people neurotic. (. . .) I fed the children and then went to wash clothes. (. . .) I was scrubbing when I heard Vera's voice calling, "Look, Mommy."

She was accompanied by two men. When they came toward me, I asked them, "What newspaper are you men with?"

"We're from the TV station and we want to invite you to be on a program. You have to be there at 8 P.M."

"Fine. I'll go."

"Bring your children."

I finished the clothes quickly and went back to the house and started to get the children ready to go. I placed the notebooks in a folder, I went around telling the people with televisions to watch me on the eight o'clock show because I was going to be on it. (. . .) The program began. My kids were delighted because they were seated on the stage. Vera was grinning. I was interviewed by a reporter named Heitor Augusto. We talked about the favela and why the favela is the garbage dump of São Paulo. It's because in 1948 when they began to tear down houses to make room for tall buildings, we poor folks who lived in those tenements were dispersed and we wound up living under bridges. That's why I refer to favelas as the city's trash heap. And we poor are the trash.

I went to sleep at 10 P.M. I was very happy.

May 8 . . . I went to the butcher's. I selected a piece of meat. That took nerve. Thanks to God, today I'm able to ask for the cut of meat I want. I looked at the bones that were on the counter and said, "You said that I write but don't earn enough even to eat. Thank God I am going to get Cr$150,000 for my book and I'll have whatever I want to eat."

I picked out another piece of meat. I paid Cr$70 I thought about the reporter [Audálio Dantas],[4] the man who allied himself with me at the most critical time in my life. Now I speak and am listened to. I'm no longer that dirty black woman from the favela. I arrived at the grocery and bought tomatoes, kerosene, eggs, and bread. (. . .) I went to make lunch. I made tomato sauce for the

ravioli and put lots of cheese on it. The children ate it and
enjoyed it. They yelled, "Viva!"

May 9 . . . Two reporters showed up. They said that they were
from *O Globo* and I asked them to come in. They asked me if I
had any trouble finding an editor. I replied that I was tired of
groveling before editors in this country, and that I had requested
that the *Reader's Digest* in the United States publish my books so that
I could have a house and food to eat; I had sent some manuscripts
but they were returned to me.

. . . Adalberto sent me some beef and bacon that Ramiro had
given me. Adalberto asked me to prepare a steak for him. What a
good thing to know that one has enough to eat. It seems that my
entire life has turned around. From hunger to plenty. (. . .) I was
straightening up the shack when Ramiro came to the window. He
said to me that he saw the newspapers and congratulated me. I
thanked him for giving me the bacon and the beef. He said that
Chessman's death had made him very sad, that Chessman had
come out of an unhealthy environment. The intellectuals had
done everything they could to stop his execution. If the United
States had pardoned Chessman they would have won the sympathy
of the whole world, because the world was watching.

May 10 I was carrying water when I heard the voice of a neighbor,
Sr. Alexandre.

"Dona Carolina, someone's here to see you!"

It was Professor Walter José Faé with his students. Professor
Faé said that many people are going to make money from what
I have done. I became happy. How nice! Even thousands can
have good come from it. The sun stands alone in the sky and
distributes its warmth to everyone.

May 12 I went to wash clothes. Dona Adelaide wants me to arrange
for her daughter to sing on television.

. . . I was ironing when I saw Dona Adelaide's son approach
with a man and tell him, "It's here."

The man asked me, "Are you Dona Carolina Maria de Jesus?"

"I am. Come in."

He entered, took off his hat, and greeted me, saying that he had read an article about me in German. He had come to meet me. He gave me a new book, *The Great Gospel of John the Evangelist.* He asked me not to relax and not to become vain or proud if I become rich, and not to be vengeful. And to help the poor. That in the world only people with humble spirits have value. For me to thank God for what he had provided me. (. . .) The name of the man who gave me the book was José Galler.

May 13 . . . Today is the day we commemorate the abolition of slavery [in 1888]. If it hadn't been abolished, I'd be a slave because I'm black. (. . .) I went to make a telephone call to the reporter. He told me to meet him at 11:30. He invited me to go with him to the theater [auditorium] of the Medical School, where there would be a celebration of the anniversary of emancipation. The spectacle would be performed by the Brazilian Popular Theater, directed by the poet Solano Trindade. (. . .) I got ready and left to meet with him at the entrance to the [offices of the newspaper] *Diário da Noite.* I didn't know that the Medical School had a theater. When we arrived, the theater was jammed. A "speaker"[5] came to narrate the scenes. The title of the show was "Afro-Brazilian Rhapsody." The performance resulted from collaboration between the Sociology Faculty and the Oswaldo Cruz Faculty on the tenth anniversary of the Brazilian Popular Theater. The poet Solano Trindade went up on the stage to speak about racial prejudice in South Africa and about the condition of blacks in the United States. He said that he had a visitor to announce, and shouted, "Carolina!"

I bounded to the stage amid applause.

. . . After the show I was introduced to some people who were on the stage and were asking for autographs. I wanted to return by trolley[6] but the reporter wouldn't let me, and he drove me back. I got out at Araguaia Street and returned to the favela.[7] It was 1:30 A.M. I was thinking about the celebration of the anniversary of the end to slavery. But we have something worse—hunger. I spoke with a black artist and he told me that he liked to

be black. Me too. I became enchanted with the black man, João
Batista Ferreira. It is lovely to be satisfied with what we are. The
favela was calm. I didn't encounter anyone. At night the shacks are
all black. Black is the existence of the favela dwellers. I opened the
door and woke up the children. They ate little pies and I went to
lie down because I was cold. I didn't sleep. I kept thinking about
the reporter.

May 14 . . . I need to wash clothes because tomorrow I'm going
on television. Today I'm happy. Everyone sees me on the street.
I've become accustomed to my new life. I went by José's bar, on
Deocleciano Street, and chatted with him. I told him that I don't
come around anymore because I don't have time. I was seen in all
the papers. (. . .) I lay down for a while because I was sleepy. But
who can sleep in a favela with so much noise? I don't know how the
favelados can be so happy in the midst of so much misery. Seeing
that I couldn't sleep, I got up. I opened the window and stared out
into space. The sky was gray, the sun covered by clouds. The piece
of sky that covered the favela was sad and gloomy. (. . .) At ten I
went out with the children. When I got close to the market I saw
crowds of people. I thought, There's a fight for sure. I saw Alfredo
running and a man from Bahia running after him with a knife in
his hand. Alfredo fell and the Bahian went to stab him. The
thrust missed, and Alfredo got up and dove into a house. The
Bahian stood in the street with the knife in his hand. I could have
taken the knife from him with a stone but I can't get involved in
these fights because I have to think of the books I intend to write.
My children mixed into the crowd. Dona Isaltina was crying. I felt
sorry for Alfredo. He is inoffensive. I shouted, "João. José Carlos,
Vera! We're going to the television station."
   . . . It was raining when we left TV Tupi. The reporter called a
cab. He intended to drop off a journalist at his house but the taxi
broke down. In the middle of São João Avenue the driver had to
get another taxi to push us. The reporter paid the fare. He gave
Cr$200 to the driver and told him to keep the change. The taxi
then took me back to the favela. The driver kept boasting that he

was rich, that he had more than two million and owned rental properties. When we arrived I looked at the meter: Cr$140. I told the cabbie, "Give me the change from the 200."

"Ah! I can't, because the journalist told me to keep it."

"You ought to give it to me."

When we arrived at the favela the driver was shocked. His glance darted from one place to another. He exclaimed, "I swear, what a place! So this is a favela! This is the first time I have seen a favela. I thought favelas were pretty places because of the samba:

> Favela, oi, favela
> Favela that stays in my heart . . .

Who would keep a place like this in his heart? While the driver was looking around at the favela I thought, Surely the samba composer had a nice woman in a favela. The driver said to me, "Look, I'm going to give you the change because someone who lives in such a place needs it more than I."

He took Cr$120 out of his wallet. When he gave it to me, I said to him, "You made a mistake with the change." He took out his wallet and gave me Cr$60.

May 16 At 7:30 A.M. the jeep from TV Record showed up. The driver was black, Sr. Elpidio Ferreira. When I got to the Channel 7 station it was quiet. The driver went to find the reporter Souza Francisco to tell him I had arrived. Souza Francisco introduced me to the illustrious Sr. J. Silvestre. He explained to me how the program would be done. . . . Sr. J. Silvestre read paragraphs from my diary. I am anxious to see this book [appear in print] because I wrote at the end of desperation. There are people who curse when they are nervous, or think of killing themselves. I write in my diary.

May 17 I dressed Vera and José Carlos and we went to the city. I went by Sr. Eduardo's shop to pay him what I owed. I told him I was going to the city to get some books. We took the bus. . . . I became happy when I saw the reporter José Hamilton. Later Sr. Gil Passarelli came. We went to 267 Carneiro Leão Street. The owner of the publishing house [Edições O Livreiro Ltda.] was standing in the doorway. He told me I could pick out the books I wanted. With the reporter watching I selected books. . . . Today is my great day. Sadness has burdened me for a long time. It came uninvited. Now the sadness has left because joy has arrived. Where will the sadness go? It must be waiting in some shack in the favela.

. . . I said goodbye and continued to look at the stores with their merchandise. The sun was hot. Today it came up at 8 A.M. I thank the sun for having awakened earlier in order to warm the workers.

. . . I can buy some clothes for myself. Everything in me is awakening. I am thinking about earrings, necklaces, pretty clothes; I'm going to see a dentist. . . . In the street the ordinary people congratulate me. When I pass near a bus I hear, "Look, it's the woman who writes!"

May 18 . . . I walked up São Caetano Street looking at the shops. The shop owner showed me several blouses. I didn't want to buy any because I didn't have enough money. She insisted so much that I agreed to buy two jackets for the children. She asked for Cr$1,700 but I only had Cr$1,500. She told me that I could take the jackets and come back with the remaining Cr$200 tomorrow; João and José Carlos put the jackets on and were happy. It was the first time they had worn jackets. João said; "What a nice thing to be the son of a poetess!"

May 19 . . . I opened the window to look at the sky. I'm used to looking to see if it looks like rain. Esmeralda's husband is nervous. We women know what these moods mean. I asked Chico if his wife has started to have labor pains.

"Since last night"

"Did you call the midwife?"

"Yes, but she didn't show up."

I saw that he was lying and went to see what was going on. Esmeralda was on her feet and crying. I looked around their sparsely furnished shack. The only things in abundance were the skinny and barefoot children. I saw that the stove was unlit. I thought, In a house with many children, by this time the beans should be cooking. The children looked sad. Where there is nothing to eat people can't be happy. The poor are the students of a teacher named hunger. I looked at Esmeralda, whose back was turned. She prayed, the strangest prayer I have ever heard. It went this way:

"My Lord Jesus: I am so poor that I have no recourse. I am with pains of labor and pain in my heart because I have nothing in my house to feed my children. I can't call the midwife because I have no money to pay her. Only you can help me, Lord Jesus."

I went out of the room and asked Chico if he had any money.

"I don't. Payday is the twenty-fourth."

"How much do you need?"

"Cr$200 would be enough."

I entered the store with a 1,000-cruzeiro note and changed it. I returned in a hurry and gave Cr$500 to Chico.

"You can pay me back when you can."

He smiled. And Esmeralda, even with her labor pains, smiled.

Her husband Chico asked a woman to go to the pharmacy to buy a syringe. She ran out and I went to see if the midwife had arrived in the favela, because the husband said he had called her. . . . I was worried about Esmeralda, thinking, If she dies, who is going to look after those children? I heard the children talking, "The baby came! The baby came!"

I heard its cry and thought of an old proverb, "Man enters the world crying and leaves it whimpering."

May 22 . . . I have to go to the television station. I washed, changed, closed the shack, and took the children. When we arrived I asked for Sr. Durval de Souza at the entryway. The doorman showed me who he was. What a handsome man! He told me that during the program I should write a message for children. I wrote it. (. . .) Sr. Vicente Leporace came to meet me. Vera was happy and said, "What a lovely house, mama. What a thing to live in such a big house! Is this house a palace?"

"Practically a palace," I responded.

"Did you see, mama?"

"See what?"

"The people here don't smell like *pinga*.[8] Don't they drink *pinga*?"

"No."

"They don't smell bad, right, mama?"

"They bathe every day."

When the program started, I went to the stage. (. . .) After Sr. Durval de Souza announced me and Sr. Leporace put makeup on me, I went up. He said that I was a major literary find. He gave me a pen made of pure gold.

. . . People in the street said, "Look at the writer who was on television."

"She got a gold pen."

"Gold!"—I heard them say—"what good fortune!"

"Why did she get the pen?"

"She's the writer from the favela."

I also heard an ironic comment, "Favelas don't make writers. They make thieves, rapists, vagrants. People who live in the favela are good for nothing."

I wanted to hear more, but Vera told me, "Let's go home; I'm cold."

And she tugged at my skirt.

June 3 . . . I'm writing and I hope to continue to write. I've achieved my dream of being able to write. I have the impression that I am traveling back to the past, returning to when I was twenty, eighteen. I loved life. I loved spring, autumn, winter and summer. Nowadays, I don't get along so well with summer. I made my peace with the spring and it adorned by heart with perfumed flowers and built a gold castle for me to live in. The castle is the reporter's heart, this generous man who is getting me out of the mud. I was alienated, I didn't believe in anyone. I hated politicians and bosses because my dream was to write but the poor can't have lofty goals.

After I met the reporter, everything became transformed. And I place the reporter on a pedestal in gratitude.

June 17 . . . In São Bento Street I stopped to chat with a newspaper vendor. He said that I was in *Ultima Hora* and showed me the paper. I bought two and read on the first page, "Carolina is going to leave the favela. She will publish three additional books. The humble colored woman from Canindé favela, living in misery with her three little children, semiliterate, began to record on paper found in the garbage the story of her years of suffering. A reporter discovered her and as a result Maria de Jesus' diary will be published before the end of the year. More books will follow. She says that her dream is to have a decent life far away from the favela."

The reporter José Roberto Penna said that I am semiliterate. This means that I am half-educated. . . . In the elevator, Vera started pushing the passengers. I told her, "Say 'excuse me.' This isn't the favela."

June 28 . . . I'm thinking, What will my book *Quarto de Despejo* be like?

The reporter arrived and asked me what was new. I didn't answer. He asked me if I wasn't afraid of the favelados because I wrote about them.

"I'm not afraid. You have to tell the truth."

The reporter told me that he wrote the preface to the book.

"Let me read it."

He let me. I read it. It fits with the entries in the book. I like the preface. . . . I showed him a new play [I wrote], "The Woman Who Lost Her Rights." He left, and a reporter named Ronaldo arrived. We talked. I told him that I should get a job on the radio. Ronaldo disagreed. He said I should write. I wanted to turn to radio, as a singer. I became furious with Audálio's authority, rejecting everything, canceling my projects, as if I were his slave. There are days in which I adore Audálio; there are days when I curse him for everything. Hangman, executioner, controller, and so on. . . . I cursed Audálio. He doesn't give me the freedom to do anything. I can sing! I can be on the radio as a dramatic actress and he doesn't let me. . . . I spent the afternoon getting ready to go to Radio Gazeta. At 5:15 I entered, looking around for Professor Faé. Some youths were talking with the doorman and asked me what I wanted. The program's director, Sr. Fernando Soares, came over and asked me to go upstairs with him. . . . The

announcer said that I was from Sacramento, that I studied two
years at the Alain Kardec School. Dona Lília spoke and recited
two poems. . . . I thanked them and said goodbye and took
the bus, thinking about what Fernando Soares had said, that I
shouldn't be a radio singer. That I should obey Audálio. I bought
some snacks for the children and took the streetcar.

July 2 . . . I went to the *O Cruzeiro* agency. The reporter wasn't
there and I sat waiting. I looked around admiringly because I had
started to like the *Diários* building. I got to know the poet Formiga
and the magazine director. At eleven, the reporter arrived,
greeted me, and said that tomorrow Cyro Del Nero would take
photographs to use in the book. He said that the second edition
would be ten thousand and the third [edition] thirty thousand
copies, and that I would earn more than Cr$500,000. He said that
I shouldn't feel vain about it. I'm not at the age to feel vain. I've
already experienced all of life's ups and downs.

He listened to me but said nothing new. . . . Dr. Elias Raide
came in to do an interview for the *Mundo Ilustrado.* The employees
left. Today is Saturday. I went with Elias Raide for the interview.

. . . I chatted with Sr. Otavio. I told him that I was going to
move out of the favela later in the month and that I don't like the
day-to-day [life there]. I don't know what they think about my
diary. I write about the misery and unlucky lives of the favelados.

July 4 . . . We went downtown. I got to the bookstore and asked
Sr. Lélio for Cr$1,000. He told me he would give me Cr$50,000
on the seventh. I insisted. Sr. Lélio was reading the galleys from
my book.

. . . The reporter told me not to tell the favelados that I
was going to get Cr$50,000. We arranged for me to be at the
bookstore at two on Thursday. . . . I went to see Sr. Rodolfo. I
went into the printing plant to talk with the workers, who were all
happy.

"Did you receive anything yet?"

"I'm going to on Thursday. I'm going to buy a piece of land,
God willing."

I don't know the employees by name. One of them said, "Are you signing checks yet?"

"Not yet. Soon I will, God willing."

"How old are you?"

"Forty-six."

"Gee . . . that's very old. Otherwise I'd marry you."

I left, humored. I spoke with the employees because I owed them thanks. They gave me money to buy food for my children.

July 5 . . . I got up at 2 A.M. and read, thinking of my life that is now transforming me. Finally I'm going to have a little house and a plot of land for the rest of my days. I'll plant flowers and raise chickens. I'll have a musician—a rooster singing cock-a-doodle-doo!

July 7 . . . I'm going to the bookstore to get my royalty money. I thought about the poor because I'm already disconnecting myself from them. But I'm not happy because I know how hard it is to be hungry. . . . When I got to the bookstore I waited in the doorway for the reporter. Passersby stopped to talk with me and ask when my book was going to come out.

. . . I entered, greeting everyone. They looked at me cheerfully. The reporter was there, Sr. Lélio, and another reporter. I greeted them.

"Where are your children?" the reporter asked.

"They went to have breakfast with the boys who work on the balcony."

Sr. Lélio gestured me over with his eyes. He told me to call for my children. I obeyed. I found them fooling around on the stairs. We got back in a hurry and I went over to the reporter.

. . . Sr. Lélio gave me the contract to read. I read that I would receive Cr$40,000 in royalties for my book *Quarto de Despejo.* I wondered about the book, some of the things I wrote so long ago to drown the miseries that were enveloping me just like the *cipó* vines that choke trees, wrapping around them.

. . . Sr. Lélio showed me to a chair. I sat down. The children, the reporter, and Sr. Lélio stood around me. The photographer

took a picture of me signing the paper and receiving the money
that had been made ready. Sr. Lélio asked the cashier [to give it to
me] and said that I should count it. I was extremely nervous when
I did it. . . . João was overcome with emotion when he saw the
1,000-cruzeiro bills. He wanted to count them but he didn't know
how.

. . . Sr. Lélio told me that I should put aside part of the
money and save another part for the down payment for a house.
To deposit in the bank. The reporter mentioned one. I said
goodbye to Sr. Lélio and we fled down the elevator. I said goodbye
to Dona Adelia and we headed for the bank. We got there, on
Fifteenth of November Street, Number 63. We started up the
steps. Several people looked at me, shocked. The reporter went to
talk with a man about opening an account. He explained that the
account would be mine. The man looked me over. He opened his
eyes slowly, showing discontent. I felt like hitting him in the face.
. . . We filled out the form and I signed. We went to the
cashier. When the teller came to my name, he read it aloud,
"Carolina Maria de Jesus!"

I was getting sick of hearing my name mentioned so often. I
gave him the money. We left the bank.

July 16 . . . I was cooking rice and lentils when Vera said to me,
"Mama, look at Audálio and Paulo [Dantas]!"

I heard the reporter's voice and looked around. I went outside
and greeted the reporter, who was with the writer Paulo Dantas.
He told me the book would be published on August sixteenth.
What a shock this gave me! I know that I am going to make my
enemies angrier, because no one is used to this kind of writing.
Whatever God wills. I wrote the truth because I thought that the
reporter would never publish it. He photographed me and said
that he was awaiting Sr. Cyro Del Nero, who would do the art work
for the book.

July 27 . . . Vera was playing with her friends and I went to lie
down. I read a book of poems. Vera called, "Mama, the reporter
is here!"

I got up, opened the window, and saw the photographer, a very pretty woman. The reporter didn't give her name. She is with the Diários Associados group of Porto Alegre. She photographed and interviewed me. She said that she would send me the *Rio Grande do Sul* newspaper she writes for. . . . I showed her the sambas I am composing and that I wanted to record. But the reporter said to me that writers cannot sing, that professions are divided: singers are singers, writers are writers. I wanted to be on the radio.

August 10   . . . I took the trolley, thinking that they should have wings. When I arrived at the Press the reporter wasn't there. The Bahian man there told me to enter and to sit down. I began to say that the reporter should let me make money by being a radio performer.

"The reporter is practical. You should listen to him."

He said that it was a good thing not to let me be on the radio. I know that journalists defend one another. I took a paper and wrote a note to leave for the reporter. [Then] he came through the door and greeted me. He held out his hand. I opened my hand and touched his hand without shaking it.

"This is a way to greet people now?"

I handed him my note to read.

"So it's this way now? Good, let's talk."

I went with him. When he arrived the other journalists changed the way they were standing around. I thought, The Emperor has arrived. I felt equal to the reporter. He was the first to speak, ... The reporter told me that I was vain.

"How vain can I be? I am seeking simply to do what is humble. I was a maid, I scavenged for paper, I live in a favela. You don't want any more humility than this."

"You should be proud of what you do."

I saw that he wanted to make me feel good—that I am a good writer. When I was at the bank, a man spoke with me and asked me when the book would appear. It will come out on the nineteenth, on Friday.

The reporter invited me to go with him to the Francisco Alves Bookstore to see the book's illustrations. . . . Sr. Lélio was sitting at his desk. He smiled when he saw us. The reporter showed me the drawings. What I liked was [the drawing of] the 1[000]-cruzeiro note, my three children, and me. And the wrapped package of rats, when the woman went begging for food.[9]

August 13 . . . I began to make lunch: rice, beans, and meat. I was writing when the pots began to boil and when the man from the publishing office came and told me that the reporter would bring my book. I felt happy.

"It's ready now?"

"Yes."

I was anxious to see it, asking God to make the reporter come. I wanted to see how the book looked. I sent João to fix up the yard. There was no chair on which the man could sit. The children took outside the box I used to seat visitors and it got stolen. I became ashamed and asked the man to sit on the bed. The shacks of the poor are always lacking something. . . . I went outside and chatted with a neighbor. I told her that the book was ready. I jumped for joy when Vera yelled, "Look, it's Audálio!"

I went inside the shack. Prof. Valter [Walter] José Faé and the famous writer Paulo Dantas came in [with Audálio Dantas]. After we exchanged pleasantries the reporter [teasingly] asked me if the book was going to come out or not. I smiled.

"How are things, Dona Carolina?"[10]

"I'm doing fine."

The reporter unwrapped the books and gave me one. I became overjoyed when I looked at it and said, "What I always envied on books was the author's name."

And I read my name on the cover.

Carolina Maria de Jesus.
Diary of a favela dweller.
QUARTO DE DESPEJO [*The garbage room*]

I was overcome. The reporter grinned, "Is everything OK, Carolina?"

"Oh, yes! Everything is OK."

You have to like books to feel what I felt. Professor Faé said, "Today is the thirteenth, a lucky day."

. . . I went to the pond to fetch my clothes because I wanted to read my book. The children got ready to sleep and lay down. I kept reading my book *Quarto de Despejo* until three in the morning. When I finished reading it I said, "God bless the reporter!"

I became so emotional that I couldn't sleep.

August 14 . . . I went to wash clothes and chatted with Dona Nenê. I told her that my book had been published. . . . I gathered some clothes and went to her house to iron them. The iron was hot. I showed her the book. She became happy when she saw her name in my book and that I had written about her giving me food to eat. I went to Dora's shack to iron the clothes. She lent me her electric iron. I showed her my book. She doesn't like to read. She looked at the book without displaying any interest.

. . . I took the trolley to the city. I carried with me a copy of the book. I went into bars and showed it.

"It's for sale already?"

"Yes, at the Francisco Alves Bookstore."

I went to the Diários Associados offices. It was cold inside, so I went back into the street and sat down on the sidewalk [to write]. An employee of the Diário came over and asked me what I was writing. I gave him my book and the reporter's preface for him to see. I told him that the reporter had helped me a lot and that I liked him also. . . . I continued writing. I jumped when I heard the reporter's voice, "This isn't a good place to write."

. . . We went to the Artistic Culture Theater for a television interview. When we arrived we met the songwriter Heitor dos Prazeres. The reporter introduced me. . . . When [the actress] Dona Bibi Ferreira arrived I went to talk with her. What a marvelous woman: attentive, cultured, as elegant as a rose's petals. The introductions continued. Sr. Cyro Del Nero designed the sets for the program. It was a representation of a favela.

. . . We remembered that I was supposed to have my children on the television program. I went back to the favela. I took the trolley. When I arrived at the last stop I showed my book to people who knew me. The reporter had given me the book yesterday and the cover was already soiled because the children grabbed it every minute. The book was already the color of the favela. I told the neighbors in the cinder-block houses that I would be on television with Dona Bibi Ferreira.

. . . When we arrived at the theater I was confused. The reporter, the children, and I went up to the stage. When the program started I was nervous. I got the name of the publishing house mixed up. I realized that it was from being tired, that I had spent all of last night reading the book. I appreciated the comments made by Dona Bibi Ferreira. She held my book in her hand during the entire program.

August 15 . . . I heated water for me to bathe. I am going to the bookstore to bring a bit of earth to put in the display window. It was raining; we went by bus, and when we arrived I saw my picture on the door. It is a drawing of me in heavy crayon. And the favela. The caption said, "This favela dweller, Carolina Maria de Jesus, wrote a book—*QUARTO DE DESPEJO*—Livraria Francisco Alves offers it to the public."

I went in and asked for Sr. Lélio. He hadn't come. And the reporter?

"He hasn't come in either."

I signed three books that Sr. Thomaz asked me to autograph. . . . The painters arrived. I told them that Sr. Cyro Del Nero is a fine painter. The man who arranged for the painting, the artist Irenio Maia, told me that he had done it and asked me if I liked it.

"It's excellent. I look good."

What a surprising thing! People and cars stop in their tracks to look at my picture. I felt as if I had gone to heaven. I told people, "I hope that you buy my book."

"Oh! it's you!"

"It's me. When I had nothing to eat instead of cursing I wrote. And the reporter made it into a book: he typed it, publicized it, and brought it to the publisher, Dr. Lélio de Castro Andrade.

The cars and buses stopped. And pedestrians. Today it is raining and the raindrops spattered on my picture.

. . . We took the trolley to Tiradentes Avenue and I went to inform Sr. Rodolfo Sherauffer[11] that my book was in print and will be sold starting on Friday the nineteenth, at 5 P.M. I will autograph copies. He asked me, "Do you need money?"

"No, sir. The editor gave me Cr$40,000. I deposited [most of the money] in the bank."

I opened my bag and showed my 1,000-cruzeiro bills to Sr. Rodolfo. I said goodbye and went down the street telling people I knew to buy my book. I went into bars where I used to have coffee. I went into the Casa Rainha to see if Sr. João Gomes was there to invite him to buy a copy. He wasn't there. I went to tell the owner of the store on the corner of Eduardo Chaves Street that my book was for sale at the publisher's bookstore. He said that he would buy one. People told me that I was dressed nicely. They said, "Just look at you now!"

I went to tell Dona Mildrede to go and buy my book. She said that she couldn't go because her husband broke his leg but that her son would go. I said goodbye to her and her children, who are handsome and decent. I went to tell Aldo about my book. Friday is the day. His mother received me warmly. The house was filled with visitors. I went to the kitchen to see Dona Iridê. I showed her the book and invited her to come to the publishing house.

I took my leave and returned to the favela. I spent the afternoon writing. I am happy.

August 16   It was raining when I woke up. Seeing the rain reminded me that I would hunt for paper even on rainy days. It was my day of bitterness, like Christ's. I've known the hard side of life.

. . . I fixed coffee; the children ate bread. Now that food is plentiful for us the children are well fed, abundantly so. They are noisier, more alert. I feel that I have awakened from a dream, one in which I suffered prison, hunger, flood, fighting.

God was charitable in not bringing us illnesses. I went to the city to show Vera and José Carlos my picture. Vera said that it was pretty. I went into the bookstore to bring a card of the Sacred Heart of Jesus, to put it in the window that was decorated like a favela. Dona Adelina, the cashier, was reading my book. She said to me, "Your book is excellent. I'm nearly finished. Your children are terrible, possessed with the devil."

I smiled and looked at my children, who were now starring in books.

August 18 I telephoned the reporter, who joked with me, "Dona Carolina Maria de Jesus, do you have a secretary now?"

I smiled and told him that I would buy some earrings.[12]

He told me that I was in the second edition of the newspaper *Diário da Noite.* I went to a store to buy a piece of costume jewelry. I hadn't gone shopping for some time. What a surprise for me! I saw beautiful things. But the prices! . . . well, I'm not going to comment on the prices. I bought something for Vera and earrings for me. I told the clerk to hurry because I had to sign autographs. That I wrote *Quarto de Despejo.*

"Ah! It was you?"

I showed her my picture in the *Diário da Noite.* She wished me well. I left and went down Praça Patriarca. The news vendor who sold me the paper said that my book was very expensive. Where I stopped people gathered to watch me as if I were from an alien world. When I arrived at the bookstore I bounded up the iron stairs. The reporters followed me.

Dr. Lélio de Castro Andrade greeted us cordially. The reporters interviewed me. The books for me to sign were brought over. The journalist Carlos de Freitas's interview went this way:

Question: "Carolina, what is your reaction to the way your life has changed?"

Answer: "I'm happy and thank all those who helped me have my book printed. It is a dream come true."

Q.: "What do you think of the elections?"

A.: "I hope that the winners work for the people, because the only time politicians care about the people is at election time. After that, they divorce themselves from simple people."

Q.: "What do you think of Fidel Castro's government?"

A.: "I adore Fidel Castro. He's is doing well defending Cuba. Countries should be independent. Every one should run its own house."

Q.: "And if you were governor, what would you do?"

A.: "I would emphasize agriculture, put land into production,

build comfortable houses for the favelados. They would work on
the land and do well morally and physically."

The bookstore employees interrupted us for me to sign
books. What happiness inside me! I was signing my book. I was
touched. They asked me so many questions that I couldn't keep
them inside my head. There were people who bought the book
and insisted on seeing me. They brought their copy for me to
autograph. The group of journalists departed. I continued
signing. The reporter arrived and asked me to sign copies for
the critics. Then we left. We went to TV Channel 5 to Walter
Avancini's program about my book.

. . . I went to talk with the journalist Dorian Jorge Freire.
I gave him a copy of my book. He told me that he had written
something about it. He showed me his column and gave me a
copy of the paper. I left because I was thinking about my children.
[The poet] Eduardo de Oliveira accompanied me to the favela. I
showed him my writing. I read some of his poems. He was pleased.
He complained about the times in his life when he was bitter. The
poet Eduardo de Oliveira said goodbye.

I cleaned up the children, made dinner, and started writing.

August 19 At 4 A.M. I started to prepare the food for lunch and
went to the spigot for water, because I had to go to the bookstore
to autograph my book *Quarto de Despejo.* I bathed; then I told the
children not to fight, and to get haircuts and come back to
the favela, and that I would come back to take them downtown to
the bookstore in the afternoon. I had breakfast and left. I went
by bus to Libero Badaró Street and bought a *kibe* to eat. When I
arrived at the bookstore it was open. I went in, darted up the stairs
and went to sign books. Sr. Nelson Assumpção treated me kindly.
The telephone rang and an employee said that it was for me. It was
the reporter Gil Passarelli. He asked me how long I was going to
stay at the store.

"Until eleven."

I went on signing copies. The reporters came and questioned
me. Audálio came and chatted with Gil Passarelli. I signed until
noon. A blonde woman, a writer, arrived, wanting to talk with the

writer Paulo Dantas. She showed him her manuscripts. He said they were beautiful, but he listened to her with anger inside him. You could sense this, but he is a writer who has to be well mannered and tolerant. She maintained that her book would be a success if it had a suggestive cover. She asked me to give her one of my books. [I said] "I can't give you a book because they are not mine. I receive a percentage of the books."

Sr. Paulo Dantas gave her a book and we left to have lunch. The reporter told me to go [to the favela] by cab. I obeyed. I hailed a taxi and told the driver to fly. We chatted.

. . . We arrived. The driver was horrified upon seeing the favela.

"What's this here, Dona Carolina?"

"São Paulo's garbage room."

"I don't believe it. Jesus![13] How can you people live here?"

"We favelados are castoffs. We have difficulty finding food to eat. We have to struggle as if we were in a war."

"And do you feel cold?"

"We feel all of life's pain."

I said goodbye to the driver, paid him Cr$130, and ran to the shack. I heard the children's voices.

"Look, it's Mama!"

I got hot water. I washed the kids and changed. I had lunch and closed up and we left. Vera wanted to go by taxi. I was wearing new shoes. . . . I asked Sr. Valentim the time.

"Three o'clock."

We took the bus. We got off at Libero Badaró Street. I was listening to comments about *Quarto de Despejo.* As soon as I entered the store I became overcome with emotion at the scene, and I went to sign books. Sr. Lélio was already there, and waiters in formal clothes went around fixing up the tables for a cocktail reception. Eyes looked at me. Dr. Lélio de Castro Andrade, my distinguished publisher, brought me over to the place to autograph the books. I didn't feel nervous amid so many people; I felt happy. My children looked the bookstore over. There were so many books for me to sign that I didn't notice the hours pass. Reporters were there, photographing me. *Ultima Hora* brought some favela dwellers to the bookstore to be interviewed. The favelados were appalled to see me, a black woman, being treated as if I were an empress.

At 4 P.M. Minister João Batista Ramos arrived. The Minister of Labor. What a handsome man! What a voice! He was anxious to leave because he had a radio program to do. Vera pushed us to be able to see the minister's face, saying; "What a handsome man!"

The minister smiled. I warned Vera not to push the minister. "Don't call me Sr. Minister! I'm João Batista."

I signed an autograph for the minister. He had difficulty leaving because of the throng. It wasn't possible to treat him more nicely. I continued signing books for the multitude.

. . . Audálio said goodbye and asked me for a hug. But my feet had fallen asleep.

Some unimportant things happened. At 9:15 the bookstore closed. Aldo paid the taxi to the favela. I got off at the trolley stop to buy bread and fish for the children. The driver was Japanese. He was repelled when he saw the favela.

"Someone as famous as you has to live here?"

I smiled at what the Japanese said. We went to bed in our clothing because we were so tired.

But I was happy.

August 20 . . . I made coffee and went to see if I was in the papers. The ones that had published the story were the *Folha* papers and *Ultima Hora*. I was in a picture with the minister, with Vera between us, smiling. People stopped and looked at me as if I were from another planet. I stopped to receive compliments from my public, who admired my courage to cite the truth.

August 21 . . . I went to meet the reporter. We went to the Ninth of July radio station. I was to be interviewed on the Student Program. I greeted the students. When I was interviewed they asked the listeners to tell them who wrote *Quarto de Despejo.* Seventy-seven people called in to say that it was Carolina Maria de Jesus. We thanked the students and went to the bus stop. We went to Correia Leite's house[14] on the Vergueiro Highway. When we arrived at Correia Leite's house I remembered the times past.

I told the reporter that I knew him. He told the reporter that he met me on Augusta Street. I was greeted warmly, everyone showing their happiness. The blacks of São Paulo were giving me their homage. Some blacks from Rio de Janeiro were there. They served lunch with the talk. I sat at the head of the table. The food was delicious. I had the impression that I was dreaming. Reporters came from the *Diário da Noite.* "Delegado"[15] made a speech. He said that the one that would set free men of color would have to come out of the garbage and the leavings.

You don't have to be cultured to understand that the cost of living is oppressing us.

August 23 . . . I went to the publisher's to sign books. The children were in their element, playing on the elevator. I admired Dr. Lélio's tolerance for accepting my children's behavior without protest. And my kids can make anyone bitter. At 6 P.M. we left the bookstore. I was anxious about arriving in the favela; I was worried that the favelados would revolt against me because I am going to become rich. . . .

When I got there I worried about an attack on me because they could think that I had the money that the magazine *Visão* said I would receive. But I didn't see any favela dweller reading *Visão* and therefore I calmed down.

. . . In the street Vera stopped at the newsstands and said, "Look at your book."

I signed books and chatted with the people. But we had to return to the city. I was going to be on a round-table discussion with intellectuals on television. Father [João] Comaru told me that he would be on the round-table.

(. . .) When we arrived at the TV station we met the councilman Italo Fittipaldi. [The writer] Fernando Góes arrived last. He did not greet me. Sr. Mario Brasini spoke about the problem of dysfunctional people. The director of social services was nervous. I became happy when I saw Father Comaru's friendly face. With his black cassock he looks like Saint Geraldo.

The writer Fernando Góes opened the debate. He said that the income of a favelado was insufficient for him to live in a decent house. (. . .) The councilman Italo Fittipaldi and a physician said that favelas are disease-ridden. Father Comaru offered a few comments about my book. [He said] That no one [should] give dead rats to beggars for charity. The fact is he never has been a favelado and he [therefore] does not know the vicissitudes of favela life. I have been a beggar. I don't know if he was trying to please people but the director of social services said that favela women need to have a more comfortable standard of living. It was the only thing he said clearly. I got up and kissed him. Audálio called my book a faithful mirror of what I see and write about in my diary.

I thanked God when Father Comaru spoke and described the way public officials ignore the unfortunate, urging that they study and learn a trade.

. . . What I know is that my book is provoking confusion. The councilman Italo Fittipaldi said that my book is comparable to *Uncle Tom's Cabin*.

The round-table ended at II P.M.

August 28 . . . I was preparing coffee when Sr. Giacomo De Camilles came. He was going to take me to Father João Comaru's church in Presidente Altino. (. . .) When we arrived, the people were in the streets wearing their Sunday clothes. They were there to participate in the lottery for houses that Father Comaru was providing for the poor. Father Comaru introduced me to the people who were there. He said that I had written a book about the degradation of favela life. He invited me to speak. I went up to the stage and said that I admired the meritorious work of Father Comaru in arranging for decent houses for the indigent. He was freeing them from the favela environment, one that destroys the moral lives of children.

. . . They started the lottery. People paid Cr$500 monthly to build the houses. The first winner was Sr. Francisco da Silva. (. . .) The last one went to Sr. Manoel Freire dos Santos. The cab driver who brought me asked Father Comaru if he could find a house for me. Father Comaru said that he was going to travel and that he had no time at the moment. Sr. Antonio Soeiro Cabral overheard this and said that he had an available room in his house, and that I could use it until I found something better. Did I want to see it? Sr. Mauricio Ferraz de Camargo took us in his car and Sr. Antonio showed me the room, the tank to wash clothes, and the electric light.

"Is it OK, Carolina?"

"Is it OK? I'll be here tomorrow!"

I was overjoyed. I told the children not to be bratty. Sr. Antonio introduced me to his wife, who was preparing lunch. I told him that I would stay a few days in his house until I could find a place. I became even happier. Finally I can leave the favela. Finally my day has arrived.

August 29 . . . I went downtown to let the reporter know that I was going to leave the favela. I got off the bus and went to the newsstand to look at the papers. When the man saw me, he said, "Look at your picture in *Mundo Ilustrado.*"

I bought a copy of the magazine and told the newsman that I would be in the magazine *O Cruzeiro*[16] on Tuesday. When I got to the office the reporter wasn't there. I waited. When he arrived, I told him to go to the bank with me to cash a check.[17] I told him that I was going to rent a room in Osasco.

. . . Tonight is the last time I'm going to sleep in the favela. I told the children that we will move tomorrow. They were happy. I told Dona Alice that I will leave the favela. I noticed that she was sad. I'm going to give her my shack. I went to pack the books. I feel contented. Finally I'm going to depart from this damned place. There will be no homesickness in the baggage I take with me.

I hired a truck to take my junk to Osasco.

August 30 I got up at 6 A.M., prepared our clothes, and got ready to pull up anchor from the favela. I made coffee and went to buy bread. I asked Chico to wait on me quickly because I was going to move.

"Where?"

"I'm going to live in Osasco."

I was making ready my sticks of furniture when the owner of Boulevard Bookstore, Sr. Paulino de Moura, showed up. He came to invite me to come to his store to autograph books. (. . .) He brought some books for me to sign. I was autographing them when Gil Passarelli, the *Folha* reporter, appeared, to photograph my move. Sr. Paulino helped me hand my stuff through the window so it could be filmed and photographed. Gil departed so that the story could appear in the afternoon paper. I went back to signing books when Sr. Pompilio Tostes came to film me. He filmed the shack from outside. Then he went inside, but there wasn't enough light. João climbed on the roof to remove some shingle boards so that light would come through.

. . . The newspapers had said that I would move to Osasco at 2 P.M. The curious people in the favela were standing around and children surrounded the shack. They did not come to help me. Dona Alice said that the boys were getting into my books. I cursed them. I breathed a sigh of relief when the driver came, Sr. Milton Bitencourt. He started to get second thoughts when he saw the crowd of favelados standing around the shack. I asked him to carry my junk to the truck. [More] newspaper people were arriving to film my departure from the favela. João had disappeared. He had climbed on the roof and fell, hurting his leg. He went to the police kiosk to get bandages. Dona Alice told me again that Dona Juana's boys were messing with my books. What chaos!

Even with the confusion I felt contented. My dream was coming true. The reporters photographed and filmed. Audálio arrived with the reporter José Hamilton. Dona Alice helped me to carry my odds and ends. I turned the shack over to her and we climbed on the truck. Me and two children, because João wasn't there. The driver was nervous. Meyri stepped forward and said, "Don't forget the poor people."

Leila[18] came forward, walking with difficulty. She came to incite the favelados against me. The driver turned on the ignition and started to move the truck. The favelados began to throw rocks. Leila became agitated and threw a stone into the truck. I watched the rocks and became frightened that they would strike Vera and José Carlos in the eye; they were already injured. What a mess! I don't know where so many people had come from to witness my departure. Chica and Nair cursed me, saying, "You're getting out of here to escape being beaten."

I replied, "I've been here twelve years and you never attacked me. You can. I'm going to live in Osasco. My address is 833 Antonio Agu Street."

Audálio and the other newspapermen were in the middle of the favelados. I feared they would be attacked. I said goodbye only to Dona Alice and Dona Eunice. Audálio wanted me to say goodbye to the favelados, shaking their hands, a gesture I refused to make.

. . . The neighbors from the cinder-block houses watched me in the truck waving my hands. But I am only going to miss Dona Isaltina. What a nice Portuguese lady! She gave food and clothes for my children. The truck stopped in front of Sr. Eduardo's store. João got into the truck and said that he had been driven [from the police station] in the Channel 9 van. I scolded him and yelled, "You shouldn't have climbed on the roof. You don't listen. You should have broken a leg to teach you to obey."

Two journalists climbed onto the truck to film my arrival in the Osasco house. I wanted to wait for Audálio. I thought he had gone a different way. The driver took off. I was thinking of Araguaia Street, where I used to hunt for paper. [We passed] The street where the packing plant gave us meat. We passed Pedro Vicente Street and went in the direction of Luz Station. The driver, Sr. Milton Bitencourt, stopped at his depot and told his friends that he would be on television. A journalist got out to make a phone call. A man who was watching us asked, "Is this garbage?"

"No, it's not garbage. I am leaving the garbage room."

I laughed at the coincidence. I was not sad. The journalist who went to make a call returned, got in the truck, and we sped off. I was sleepy and thought about the delicious feeling I would have being able to lie down and sleep without noise, without hearing the drunken voice of Adalberto. I chatted with the journalists about favela life. I looked at my dirty children with their faces cut by the rocks thrown by the favelados. I had to leave the favela.

. . . When we got to Osasco I paid the driver, Milton Bitencourt, Cr$2,000. It was sacred money for me because I was paying for his work in removing me from the favela. The television people were waiting. They photographed me next to the sticks of furniture that I had found in the rubbish. I looked at the junk and thought about the fifteen years that I had lived in the garbage. I became sad because Audálio wasn't there: could it be that he didn't want me to move out of the favela?

Several people had said that Audálio had transformed me into a rat for the cats. But the rat runs faster than the cat. I ran to Osasco. Sr. Cabral's neighbors congregated, asking, "What happened?"

They were astounded at the collection of newspapermen.

"This is Carolina, who is moving to Osasco."

"The one who writes? Ah, I know."

The reporters José Hamilton and Gil Passarelli arrived. I asked where Audálio was.

"He couldn't come."

He didn't want to come. I thought, He is enigmatic and likes to be treated with flattery. But I'm not going to bow down to him. The photographers took pictures of Sr. Antonio Soeiro Cabral handing me the key. He loaned me a bed. Every one of his gestures revealed his cultural level, ways of acting that I never saw in the place I had just left. I went to get my broken-down furniture. The reporters left. I was tired. I fixed the beds and washed the children, who stood admiring how hot water came out of the shower. They smiled under the water. They ate cold meat with bread and lay down. They were exhausted.

We lay down and slept. What a luscious dream. The electric light illuminated the room. João smiled because now he could read whenever he wanted to. I woke up during the night and thought about my tragic life. People are born and as things go on life brings its trials.

Now I am in the living room.[19] Where I had always yearned to be. Let's see how my life will be here in the living room.

August 31 I spent the day in Osasco. I washed the dirty clothes. Sr. Antonio Soeiro Cabral got food at a restaurant for me. What friendliness! And so much food!

I am going to prepare my clothes because tomorrow I am going to Santos to sign books at the Recanto do Livro Bookstore.

Sr. Antonio Soeiro Cabral bought the newspapers that wrote about my being stoned when I left the favela. Something I expected: rocks are the confetti of favela dwellers.

I was struck by how Audálio didn't show up in Osasco. Could it be that he wanted me to stay in the favela?

September 1 I got up at 5 A.M. to get the children ready to go to Santos. It was raining. We went downtown by train because the children said they wanted to ride on a train.

"What's it like to go on a train?"

They didn't answer.

"Didn't I say that someday you would ride on a train?"

When we got to the station we took a taxi to the Francisco Alves Bookstore. Sr. Thomaz Parrilho was the cab driver who took me. People were asking me why the favelados had stoned me. . . . All eyes stared at my face. Sr. Thomaz Parrilho bought the tickets and we left. The bus was extremely crowded. My kids stared at the streets of São Paulo and at the luxurious houses. Each one more beautiful than the other. At Ipiranga they saw the museum and the monument and Emperor Dom Pedro I's house. I thought that the house was simple and ugly. We sang on the bus.

When we arrived in Santos it was raining. We took a cab and drove to the Recanto do Livro Bookstore. Sr. Osvaldo de Oliveira greeted us politely and drove us to the Municipal Legislature. I was greeted by councilmen. I was enchanted by the luxury of Santos's legislature. I was introduced to the vice-mayor who greeted me cordially. We were served coffee. (. . .) We went to the Recanto do Livro to sign my book. At 5 P.M. we were driven to the Ebony Athletic Club. I was nicely received by the directors. All blacks.

We left the Ebony for the bookstore. I autographed the rest of the books and went to find a bus. We couldn't find one. I hired a cab to take us to Osasco. Vera slept in the car.

September 2 I got up at 7 A.M. We changed clothes and went to the city by train. The children, who kept on insisting that we travel by train, have now become bored with it. I thought, There are people who crave something and then when they get it they grow tired of it.

When we got to São Paulo I went to the bookstore to sign copies. What a burden: all to care for my children. We lunched at a restaurant. I signed more books until 5 P.M. I said goodbye and we returned to Osasco. These days I've gone around too much. What confusions in my life. Pictures of me in the newspapers every day, people congratulate me and ask me to continue writing. The kids protest that they don't like the food served in bars.[20] I'll cook for them.

September 3 Sr. Antonio Soeiro Cabral talked with me this morning. He is horrified that Audálio didn't accompany me out of the favela.

It's that all Audálio does is write and he has no time to find a house for me. I got the children ready and we went downtown. Several people stopped and asked if I were the author of *Quarto de Despejo.* They praised the book. I am happy because I haven't heard any negative comments. I walked in the streets and the people said, "Look at the writer."

. . . We went to the *O Cruzeiro* offices. Audálio told me that I would be interviewed by a reporter from *Laife* [*Life* magazine]. Sr. George Torok gave me some cartoon drawings for my family. They were contented and looked at Sr. George Torok affectionately. We said goodbye and returned to Osasco. We took the train.

I carry the burden of a tired, troubled life, but my efforts are compensated by the fact that my book is a best-seller.

. . . I went to see the reporter. He told me I'd receive my money from the first edition on the fifth. I can say, then, "The fifth is the day!"

September 4 I'm not going out. I chatted with Sr. Antonio Soeiro Cabral about the conditions under which we live. He said that he'd come with me tomorrow to the bookstore. I'm tired. I spent the day washing clothes. I appreciate Osasco because of its tranquillity and its clean air. It seems like I left hell and am in heaven. The neighbors see me and smile. There are fewer children [around] because they don't live in the streets.

September 5   I rose at 6 A.M., made breakfast for the children, bought bread, cooked lunch, and we went downtown. I'm content. I want to organize my life. At the publisher's I stood in the doorway waiting for Sr. Cabral to arrive. He came at noon. I introduced him to the bookstore employees and told them, "This is the man who gave me a room in Osasco."

We took the elevator to the third floor. I introduced him to Dr. Lélio de Castro Andrade. He asked Dr. Lélio why he didn't take me out of the favela before the book was ready to be published. Sr. Cabral told me that I should deposit the royalties in a bank and take charge of my own money.[21]

He selected Bank I. . . . Audálio wasn't there. I had telephoned to let him know that Dr. Lélio was already present. Dr. Lélio decided to pay me without Audálio being there. Sr. Antonio Soeiro [Cabral] said that he had no intentions of interfering in my business matters. He observed that I cannot live like I am living now, and that he did not approve of Audálio's failure to visit me in Osasco.

I asked him to take the money because I am afraid of walking around with large sums of money. He telephoned for a friend to come to the bookstore to accompany us and to be a witness when I made the deposit. He named the places where he had worked. Audálio showed up. I introduced Sr. Antonio Soeiro Cabral. He said that the money should be deposited in Bank I. . . . Audálio did not object.

When I walked through the streets people recognized me. In the bank I was introduced to Sr. Antonio Soeiro Cabral's brother. He counted the money. I held out Cr$20,000 to spend. I was given a checkbook and became emotional, because I didn't expect to make so much money this way. João looked at the money and smiled. Vera displayed her joy and said, "Now I have money to buy shoes."

The manager gave me my deposit slips. "Bank I . . . Inc., Series B. #864,081 to 864,090," they read. "Note: these checks may only be used by the account holder." I deposited Cr$176,000.

Dr. Lélio gave me an accounting of the royalty payments for the first edition of my book *Quarto de Despejo* [10 percent of] 10,000 copies at Cr$24 each."

    10,000
    x 24
    ─────
    40,000
    200,000
    ─────
    240,000

This is the total I received for my book. The favela gave enormous troubles but a marvelous end.

We left the bank and went to the newspaper office. Audálio was speaking with Sr. Antonio Soeiro Cabral. I wanted to hear what they were saying but I had to watch my kids who were in back of me.

At the office I met the reporter David St. Clair [Carolina's English-language translator] who was going to do a story about me for *Laife*. He asked me questions; He asked me where I was born. Sr. Antonio Soeiro Cabral stayed in the room to hear the reporter's questions. What a reporter! I had the impression that I was in the presence of a judge.

We arranged to go to the favela the next day for me to be photographed. I said goodbye. I went with Sr. Antonio Soeiro Cabral. He paid for the taxi to Osasco.

September 6 We took the trolley. When I arrived at the office I met the reporter David St. Clair. I asked him why he is called St. Clair, which is a French name. He said that he was English. We took a cab and went to the favela. We passed by the police kiosk to request that the captain provide two officers to accompany us into the favela.

The police official was polite and assigned two policemen to us. Vera was happy because she was wearing a new dress. She went to find Dona Alice, the first woman I greeted. I went to see my shack. Dona Alice had dismantled the little room in which my children had slept. (. . .) The photographer George Torok took pictures. When the news went around that I was in the favela, the favelados all came. Audálio told me not to say anything to Leila. She was the one who instigated the favelados to stone me.

. . . Audálio and St. Clair went to see her. The favelados went along. Leila received them badly. Joaquim stared at me with an astonished look. Adalberto staggered with his walk crippled by nutritional deficiency. . . .

The reporter took us to a *churrascaria* [restaurant for grilled meats] on the Duke of Caixias Avenue. They served many plates of food. José Carlos spilled *guaraná* soda on his bread. I thought about the favelados while I ate that elegant food. I arrived at the conclusion that people from the "living room" do not suffer, and, if they do, their difficulties are minor. I yelled at the children to behave themselves at the table. Vera was happy because she is vain. She looked at the tables with their starched white cloths and smiled. João was happy because the tragic aspect of our life had vanished. Now he knows that he will eat lunch and dinner every day.

My children's mischievous behavior confused me. But St. Clair told me, "Children are the same everywhere in the world."

. . . I was returning to Osasco to leave the children because I had to return to the city to go to the Law School. The reporter David St. Clair went with me. (. . .) He thought that I lived far from the city. He was horrified when he saw the little room in which I am living. We came back in the same taxi. The reporter David St. Clair said that he would take me to the United States after I publish another book. When we arrived downtown he said goodbye, saying that he was going to buy cloth to make a topcoat for protection in wintertime. He is going to the United States for Christmas. There, at Christmas, there is snow. He is going to visit his mother. He said that he hasn't seen her for four years. She is very nice. He went on ahead and I lost him in the crowd.

I went to the offices of *O Cruzeiro* to speak with the reporter. He was writing. At seven we went to the Law School. We met the writer Paulo Dantas. When we arrived, the students were waiting for us. They made rows for us to pass. I was introduced in the auditorium. Marvelous!

Sr. Valdir, the president of the University's Academy of Letters,[22] presented me to the audience and said that I would be awarded an honorary degree. This diploma was reserved for the writer Jean Paul Sartre. But, since the French author was very busy and couldn't come, they decided to give it to me. And he said, "France has Sartre, and we have Carolina!"

Looking at the youthful audience made me feel pain for them. I thought of all the world's calamities. The cost of living is the curse of everyday life. The other curse is war because it decimates young people. War must be abolished from the face of the earth. Men have to resolve their problems by bringing about peace.

Various officials were present and the hall was filled to capacity. Audálio made the introduction. . . . The students asked about life in the favela. I answered. I said that favelados struggle to feed themselves. One asked why I, a black person, was receiving a diploma from the academy.[23]

[The questioner] was booed. They told him that racial prejudice is not tolerated. They asked me who I would vote for.

"I haven't decided yet."

Sr. Valdir closed the party. It was a party for me. I thought about the confusion of my life. I don't have an elementary school diploma but I have [an honorary] one from the São Paulo Law School. To the academic community, the future defenders of the law, I give my eternal gratitude. I hope that their world will be better than the present one. We live with anxiety because of the dangers of the age. I will enumerate them:

1. Hunger, caused by the high cost of living.
2. Because of the cost of living poor people cannot find decent housing. They have to live in favelas.
3. War. War benefits no one. It decimates countries, impoverishes the world, and extinguishes millions of precious lives. The cities are bombarded and the bombs

destroy everything. After the war ends everything has to be rebuilt.

When I said farewell to the students I felt moved. Dona Brasilia Pagani gave me a package. She was content in this cultured setting. I thought, Is it possible that among these educated people there is peace and harmony? Are these people good or are they perverse? The Law School building was filled to capacity. On the streets the students passed out fliers that said, "This School, which previously [acted to] free the slaves, needs to free the favelados."

September 9:   Vera said, "Now we are rich because we have enough food to fill our bellies."

And she laughs. Seeing her smile I feel contented and think about God. He has written another script for me to act out on life's stage. The other script was to live in the favela and listen to the song composed by the cost of living: "I am hungry."

I turned on the radio to hear what time it was because today I'm going to Mestre Jou's bookstore to autograph copies of my book. I took the bus. I was horrified seeing the sacrifice the workers make to be able to get to work.[24] Some stand the whole way, others sit. When they arrive at work they are already exhausted. (. . .) A worker's life is hard. With a capital H.

. . . When I arrived Mestre Jou was waiting for me. He told me that I was going to the bookstore on Augusta Street.[25] When I arrived I saw that a window had been prepared with my book featured and a sign announcing my presence. I signed books until 10 P.M.

September 10:   . . . Today I'm going to sign books at [another] shop on Augusta Street at the invitation of Sr. Giacomo de Camillis's sister. When I got there it was 8:30 A.M. I started signing copies. At noon I was leaving but a youth arrived and asked me to sign a book for him. He told me his name: Eduardo Suplicy Matarazzo.[26] He invited me to come to his house for lunch. I accepted the invitation. He telephoned his sister, Marina Suplicy Matarazzo, to pick me up with her car because he was on his motorbike. The owner of the bookstore offered me money but I declined. What impressed me was a woman who worked in the bookstore. She speaks seven languages and sings and plays the piano. She is Egyptian. She told me that she is descended from the Pharaohs, that she used to live in opulence. She described her castles and servants. But politics brought her financial ruin. [Her people] are refugees and have lived in many countries and she learned their languages. When an English person arrives she speaks English with them; when a Russian shows up, she speaks in Russian. She is a widow and has to work in order to live. She is unhappy with her life. She asked me to help her get a job on television. And she gave me her card.

The car came for me. I said goodbye and went to the mansion on Paulista Avenue. I chatted with the young Marina Suplicy Matarazzo, who told me about the beautiful qualities of her mother, who has eleven children. [She said] That she is very circumspect and is good to [Marina's] father. She admires her father for having the courage to raise eleven children. This father is a hero.

After we arrived at the lovely residence of Sr. Paulo Suplicy I was flabbergasted at the pictures. What pictures! I was introduced to Dona Filomena Suplicy Matarazzo, I saw her daughter-in-law and other children who were arriving. (. . .) Sr. Coriolano de Araujo Goes was present. When they said his name at the table, I was surprised and asked him, "Then you are the person who was *comissário* [mayor] of Rio de Janeiro."

He said he was. We spoke about his effort. He was distressed by the high cost of living faced by the poor.

. . . The meal was excellent. Dona Filomena showed me her house and her servants. Blacks and whites. The cook is black, and Sr. Paulo Suplicy told me that he likes her very much because she is always cheerful and trustworthy.

I said goodbye to Dona Filomena because I needed to speak with the reporter. Sr. Eduardo Suplicy got ready to take me to the Francisco Alves Bookstore. When we arrived the bookstore had closed [at midday] because it is Saturday. I showed my window display to Miss Marina, who was shocked, because she didn't know about the plight of the poor.

September 17 I don't have time to write in my diary because I have received so many invitations to visit cities in the interior to autograph books. I accept these willingly because I will get to know various cities in Brazil. I'm tired. I don't have time to read. The reporter told me that this enthusiasm of the public will pass.

I went to sign books in Mogi das Cruzes. (. . .) Sr. Antonio Soeiro Cabral doesn't complain about our staying in his house. On September 17 I went with the reporter to [the city of] Baurú. On August [September ?] 21 I moved to Antonio Agu Street, Number 908; I bought furniture for the bedroom, kitchen, and living room. . . . The patio was filled with garbage. The owner of the house, Sr. Victor, admired me for working [to clean it] with such spirit. I received a visit from the journalist Renato from the *Gazeta*. He told me that I shouldn't accept the publisher's demands that I sign books, that I am not obliged to do this. He left a card for me to look him up on Baron de Itapetininga Street.

The house was a mess. I looked for someone to help me. José Carlos arranged for a white woman, Dona Helena. (. . .) When I went to Sorocaba she didn't watch my children. Vera stayed with a woman whom I paid Cr$200. I went to Sorocaba with Professor Paulo Breda Filho. What a pleasant man! We went by car. He drove. I kept looking at the haunting landscapes and the grape orchards in the vicinity of São Roque. There are many restaurants alongside the road. I counted forty-five churches and chapels on the roadside. The inhabitants here have no distractions besides religion. For this reason the people who farm here are humble. The restaurants on the highway advertised chicken. Dr. Breda Filho took me to one of them for lunch. The woman who owned the restaurant looked at me oddly. To reassure her I told her that she had seen me on television. She remembered, and said, "Carolina Maria de Jesus, the woman who wrote a book!"

Sr. Paulo Breda Filho said that the greatest wine-producing region in São Paulo was São Roque. He ate his chicken without paying it much attention while I devoured mine avidly. He offered me wine, but I refused because I don't want to befriend alcoholic beverages.

We arrived at 3 P.M. I went to the Gutierrez Bookstore. I was received with applause and started to autograph books. I gave an interview on the radio. We went to the Rubino de Olivieira Academic Center [School], which was completely filled. I was applauded. Dr. Paulo Breda Filho introduced me. I was happy because I was not hungry. (. . .) After the presentation I signed the visitors' book. I found the signature of [Emperor] Dom Pedro II.

The debates were animated. We spoke about the problems faced by favelados. A man donated ten lots of land to be given to favela dwellers.

I slept at the Monteiro Lobato Institute [for orphans]. Boys only. Some are orphans, others are abandoned by their parents. I thought about the infamy of a mother who abandons her child. Dona Avelina Garcia is the manager of the orphanage.

. . . In the morning I went to see the children. I was impressed by the morning meal served to the children: milk and buttered bread. (. . .) Dona Avelina showed me around the inside of the orphanage. She cultivates fifteen alqueires[27] of land. She plants rice and beans. She asked me to help her get a tractor. I promised to help. I thought about men in earlier days, having to rely on their own hands. These men of the past provided for themselves with the sweat of their brows. Nowadays there are machines. Harvesting is easier.

Now that harvesting is easier, there is therefore no reason to raise the prices on food products.

I went to the laundry. Two women were washing the children's clothing. They were boiling them. I looked at the two women. I had the impression that they were two skeletons working. I greeted them but they ignored me. Dona Avelina told them that I am a writer. They listened and said, "Hum! Hum! Hum!"

I opened my purse and gave them a 1,000-cruzeiro note. I told them, "It's for you."

[They] stopped abruptly and looked at the 1,000-cruzeiro

bill. Then they looked at me and smiled. I thought, Ah, money
. . . a diabolical invention that enslaves but also frees men.

. . . I had to return to São Paulo to go to the Spring Dance in
the Fazano Party Room. (. . .) We went by bus because there were
no taxis. The drivers were on strike. When I arrived I was stunned
by the luxurious elevator in the club. It was larger than my former
shack. The staircase is covered with velvet and the tables are
adorned with flowers. Sr. George Torok's wife was cheerful. I
counted three white women. Everyone looked at my table. The
reporter arrived late. Sr. Silva Neto, reporter from *Manchete*,[28] was
good-humored and attentive. I was happy when the reporter came.
They started the coronation ceremony for the queen [of the
dance]. I crowned the queen, Miss Ester Brasil. And Sr. Silva
Neto crowned the princess. Dona Aparecida de Campos toasted
the queen. I was the object of attention for all eyes because of my
book. My fatigue lifted. I got to know the director of the Fidalgo
Club.

. . . I was in Baurú with the reporter. I was received nicely by
the councilman and the illustrious poet Nidoval Reis. What an
admirable man. We had lunch at the Country Club. What a
magnificent club! A photographer accompanied us. We went to the
Municipal Legislature and to the television station. (. . .) I was
disturbed by the airplane trip. I had the impression that I was in
[outer] space. I wasn't hungry when I went to eat but I saved some
pieces of chicken to eat if I got hungry.

. . . I spent Sunday morning at the house of the poet Nidoval
Reis. His illustrious wife prepared lunch for us. But what a lunch!
(. . .) At noon we went to the air field. The poet Nidoval went with
us and photographed us next to spring flowers. I looked at the red
ones, my favorite color. I saw land stretching in the distance. What
an immensity of land my Brazil has. It shouldn't be necessary to
have favelas in this country, nor such a high cost of living.

We went to sit outside while we waited for the airplane. I spoke
with the people who were there and recited some verses. I was
frightened when I heard the noise of the airplane. My heart leaped
like a bladder when air goes out of it.

We said goodbye to the poet Nidoval Reis and boarded the airplane. He hesitated. And I cursed the thought [as] I told myself, I won't ever write anything more! I'm going to return to the land! I thought of all the people who died in airplanes. Dom José Gaspar de Afonseca e Silva, Dr. Casper Libero, the journalist Benjamin Soares Cabello, and others. Carole Lombard. [But] The reporter reassured me. The return trip was worse because there were many clouds. What a relief when I saw the sign "Fasten your Safety Belts." Finally we arrived in São Paulo.

. . . I went to catch the bus to Osasco. The children griped that the neighbor in the back beat them because they jumped over the wall. The fact is my neighbor is just a quarrelsome person. They can't reach his wall. The man cursed at my children. He called them vagabonds who are accustomed to eating food from garbage cans.

I didn't worry about such confusions.

. . . I was in Baurú on September 24, and in São José dos Campos on the seventeenth. I autographed books, visited schools, and was greeted with fanfare. My kids were impressed. I visited a girls' school and recited. The one who accompanied me was Dr. Alvaro Gonçalves. What a distinctive black man!

I met the journalist Mauricio Loureiro Gama. He invited me to be on his program "Extra Edition," on television.

Time magazine on September 26 published a story about me on page twenty. The reporter David St. Clair wrote it. (. . .) I received an invitation to the Black Cultural Association in the Martinelli Building on the day of the Mãe Preta.[29] I got a tea set. The members of the Experimental Black Theater sang a samba for me.

I live now at 908 Antonio Agu Street. The house is in the rear. Two bedrooms and a kitchen.

I am going to start writing diary entries every day because my agitation is receding.

October 16 I got up at 5 A.M. I lit the gas stove and made coffee. The children are eating little. They changed their clothes. Today they are going to the movies. Dona Rosa, a teacher (and the owner of the Grenat Salon), came to visit me. She wrote a story about a student of hers and gave it to me to read. It is very pretty. She wrote it about ten years ago.

. . . I went to the market to buy shirts for the children. I didn't find ones that I liked. I bought a trinket for Vera because we are going to Rio tomorrow. I bought a newspaper to see how my book is doing. It is in first place.

October 17 . . . A man came to ask me to write some verses that he could record; he is unemployed. Just as I overcame the obstacles in my life, he wants to also. He is a composer. I gave him some verses to sing. He sang. He has no ear for rhythm. I figured out that he is the type who wants things easy. They forget that man, to succeed, has to attempt every kind of hard work imaginable.

October 19 . . . Some critics claim that I was too graphic when I wrote—"the children attended to their toilet"—for example. Can it be that this kind of prejudice exists even in literature? Blacks have no rights to classical usage?

October 21 I rose early and wrote until the sun came up. I made coffee and went to buy milk for the children. They attended to their toilet. (. . .) I was fixing up the house when black Roberto showed up. He is unemployed. I gave black Roberto Cr$1,000 because he wanted to commit suicide. What a low thing! A man who is strong physically and weak in his resolve.

October 24 . . . At eleven Rubens arrived. He told me that he arranged for a loan from his uncle of Cr$170,000 and wants me to lend him Cr$180,000 so he can buy a truck. A [used] truck costs Cr$350,000. I never borrowed money from anyone. I only asked for bread for my children and for leftovers.

. . . I said that I was putting aside money to buy a house or a lot because things were getting worse and I wanted to have land to plant things. He told me that he found a job and that he needed Cr$3,500 as a bond. João told me not to give him any money.

October 26 . . . The reporter invited me to go with him to the bank. My account is #36,427. I deposited Cr$150,000. We chatted

with the bank employees. They congratulated me. We left and
went to the press. I was talking with the reporter. We spoke about
Vera's father. He is going to give me a pen. I want two. One for the
reporter.

"Now he wants to give pens?"

The door opened and David St. Clair and another man
came in.

"Oh!" I exclaimed happily. And I embraced David St. Clair.

. . . I proposed to David St. Clair that we go to the bookstore.
He'll be writing an article. I said goodbye to the reporter and left
with David St. Clair. When people stopped I introduced them to
David St. Clair and said, "He is a reporter for *Time.*"

He smiled. I presented him at the bookstore on Praça Ramos.
We stopped to buy a copy of the *Tribuna da Imprensa,* but it was sold
out. We arrived at the bookstore and I introduced him, "This is
the reporter from *Time.*"

. . . We left the bookstore. We said goodbye and he said to me,
"In Rio you are going to dine with me."

October 27 . . . We went to Television Channel 2 to see Dona
Suzana Rodrigues who invited me to be on her program. We sat in
the waiting room. I chatted with the illustrious ladies who were
present. We spoke about how my life had been transformed. The
women said:

"You should adore the reporter. What a good man!"

"He did everything for you for free, didn't he?"

"He did. What I earn in a month he earns in six months.
There are days in which the reporter says that he didn't earn much
and I tell him, 'I'm sorry I can't say the same.'"

The women grinned. Dona Suzana Rodrigues told them that I
have more money than she has. I showed them my bank deposit
receipts. She told me to be careful.

"There's no danger."

. . . I told her that when I receive Cr\$100,000, I also receive
200,000 headaches. I am making both friends and enemies
unhappy because I cannot satisfy certain impossible requests.
Some want houses, some want trucks. It seems that everyone wants
something but I can't produce it. I have to fight for my children.

October 28   I got up at 7 A.M. because I went to bed late. I prepared
the morning meal. Bread, coffee with milk, and oat porridge.
How nice it is to have food to eat. I buy greens, eggs, and fruits.
My skin is becoming healthy, and I'm gaining weight.

. . . I asked João to sweep the house and the patio. He doesn't
want to. He's nervous because I told him that I'm going to marry
David St. Clair.

"You marry David St. Clair and he'll get the money from the
books. The law gives the husband inheritance rights and I want to
inherit your book royalties."

I was appalled. My son knows the laws of the Civil Code better
than I.

October 29   . . . When João becomes angry with me he proceeds this
way. If I ask him to do something he says he doesn't like me. I ask
why he treats me this way. It's because I joked with him that I was
going to marry David St. Clair and he doesn't want me to. He
ordered me not to talk about getting married, that I'm old and
very ugly.

A woman named Arlete visited me. She said she was a friend of
Dona Rosa—more than a friend. . . . She said that Dona Rosa is
rich but not charitable. (. . .) The woman said that she had been
married but was separated from her husband. She goes to work
and leaves her daughters with the servant. She is from Recife. She
went there by plane; she likes to go by plane. I told her that I am
going to travel to Rio de Janeiro. I'm going by bus. I like it
because of what I see on the way. (. . .) I thanked God when the
woman left.

. . . I have not yet become accustomed to these people visiting
me from the [city's] living room, a room where I am looking for a
place to sit.

October 30   I got up at five to prepare things, because today I'm
going to the party at the newspaper *Ultima Hora,* in Alto do
Ipiranga. I made lunch and dressed the children.

Dona Rosa and Juvenal are going to the party. I'm going with
pleasure because it is a newspaper's party. Juvenal was the first to
arrive. After him Dona Rosa arrived. A man and a boy came to

visit me. I spoke with them on the bus. He says that he admires my book. (. . .) When we got off the bus I took Juvenal to the bookstore to see my window and its display of my old and dirty notebooks. He liked my picture.

. . . When we arrived at the museum we saw no sign of any party. I asked a guard where the party was. He said, "At the Monument [to Brazilian independence]."

We went there. The children wanted to see the house of [Emperor] Dom Pedro. Vera asked the guard, "Sr. Guard, is Dom Pedro in?"

The guard smiled and said, "He is traveling."

She ran to me saying, "Mama, the guard said that Dom Pedro was traveling."

We entered Dom Pedro's house and the children were impressed with its simplicity. An oil lamp, leather bags, the beds, the harnesses, the saddles. Objects from a distant age. Brazil was poor then because our gold was shipped to Portugal. Today Brazil is poor because the receipts produced by the country do not go into the Treasury. They go into the pockets of bad politicians who do the same thing day in and day out.

We left Dom Pedro's house and went to the Monument. We saw the tent for *Ultima Hora*. The journalists began to come over to greet us. The artists [musicians and dancers] arrived but stayed mixed with the public, because the D.D.P. [the state agency for public festivities] wanted to keep the place calm. The head of the party committee went to talk with the director of the D.D.P., leaving the people to wait. We were the guests of *Ultima Hora*. If they are arrested, the public would go with them. I saw that *Ultima Hora* was loved by the people and through this process of sponsoring public festivities it makes more and more friends. A nice gesture by *Ultima Hora*, because the cost of living prevents people from being able to attend theaters.

I was horrified to see "Miss Law" interfere with an inoffensive festivity.

When the speaker introduced me on the stage I said that my dream was to see the cost of living be affordable to everyone; we have to struggle together to defeat this predicament.

The artists came up to the stage after the director of the

D.D.P. gave his permission. He agreed to do so because of the large crowd there. (. . .) [The actress] Ruth de Souza told me that she wants to make a film about my book. I told her that the person that takes care of everything like this is the reporter.

"I'll ask him."

I left and returned with the reporter. He admitted that he was preparing the script and would like to have her. She gave her address to the reporter. She was happy and thanked him.

. . . The group from the Experimental Black Theater sang the samba "Quarto de Despejo."

November 1 . . . João had dental work done. When he finished eating he looked in the mirror to see if any of the gold came out. He thinks he is important. It is his innocence. I feel pain for my children.

. . . I'm going to cook beans. The children don't eat if they don't have beans. Beans for them are a sumptuous dish. When Vera sees food, she sings.

November 2 I got up at 3 A.M. to write and read a little because I have no time during the day. Because my children act up so much. José Carlos says, "João, you need to behave better so you don't upset mama. She has a heart and the heart is the human body's clock. That clock can stop one day. It is a clock that you can't wind up."

I spent the day taking care of the children's clothing, because on the seventh we are going to Rio de Janeiro. I didn't know that today was a holiday [the stores were closed on All Soul's Day] but my neighbor gave me the honor of buying from her milk, bread, and sugar.

I opened the front door and saw the good people of Osasco going through the streets carrying flowers for their loved ones who have left this world forever. The way the world is going, the day will come when we have to say, "Long live the dead!"

November 4 . . . In the morning I was visited by Sr. João José Fech, an economist. He wanted to propose that I invest in a factory he was going to open. It is an umbrella factory. I have no money for investments. The only thing I want is to buy a little house. I know how to do business but I don't want to because my business is books.

Sr. João told me that he is married to a Jewish woman, that the Jews are united and will help one another. They are united because they follow the laws of Moses, who advised them to remain united.

November 6   . . . Dona Rosa came to visit me. I invited her to come with me to the television station. (. . .) I wanted to send the children to the movies but they are very bratty. I heated water to wash them and prepared supper for them. I changed and we left. Sr. Joaquim Rosa went with us but he didn't go the whole way because he said he felt cold. (. . .) When we arrived at the television station I met some people I knew. The notable Hélio Souto was very courteous. I told him to ask the reporter to give him a story I had written—"Felizarda"—for him to read on the radio. I summarized the story for him. Using a string from which he hung old clothes, he made the place look like a favela. Dona Carmelia Alves sang a samba to open the program. I saw that my book had many by-products. I feel contented. The television [program] was animated. Sr. Hélio Souto praised my book and offered some comments. I said goodbye to the artists and to Sr. Hélio Souto. When we arrived in Osasco it was II P.M. I took leave of Dona Rosa and went inside. I had to pack my bags, because tomorrow I am going to Rio.

November 7   We woke up at three in the morning. I told João to turn on the radio to find out what time it was. It was 3 A.M. I made coffee and João went to change clothes. I woke up José Carlos and Vera. We locked the house and went to the bus stop.

. . . The bus carrying workers to town was overloaded. It was a real headache just to get a suitcase on board. Some were seated, others were riding standing up. They were complaining that my suitcase was taking up too much space. I said that I was going on a trip.

"Where are you going?"

"To Rio."

"Where are you going to stay?"

"At the Serrador Hotel."

The jovial black man that was talking to me smiled. The echo of his laughter got the attention of everyone else. He continued asking me questions.

"Anybody staying in the Serrador Hotel wouldn't be traveling by bus. A person staying in the Serrador Hotel would be going there in a Cadillac."

The passengers smiled.

"I lent the money I would have used to go by car to a man who is unemployed."

The black man kept on talking. He told anecdotes and the passengers smiled. When we reached the downtown area we headed for the bookstore. The suitcases were heavy. The bookstore was closed. I knocked but nobody came to the door. Sr. Assumpção heard the noise the kids were making, came downstairs, and opened the door, telling me that he knew I was going to Rio. Dr. Lélio de Castro had left three tickets.

. . . We took a taxi. I paid Cr$38. At the Auto-Omnibus Company I was recognized by several people. I greeted them and went on writing my poem "May Brides" that I was going to read on TV in Rio. When we got on the bus we had a problem. José Carlos wanted to sit by himself but we only had three seats. I told the bus driver, "If you make me get off the bus I'll go back to Osasco and I won't show up in Rio. And the reporters in Rio are waiting for me."

Finally we decided I should tell the ticket taker that Vera was five years old. I opened my purse, said I could buy a ticket for Vera, and took out a 1,000-cruzeiro bill. The passengers took their seats and the bus left. Vera wanted to sit by the window. I cursed at her because my nerves were worn to a frazzle. We saw the streets that I used to roam looking for paper. It had become a habit: when I go along a street I look to see if the trash cans are out in the street. A person who rummages through trash cans is not stealing.

As we went down Tiradentes Avenue I saw some familiar places. I looked at Sr. Rodolfo's house with love and affection because he helped me a lot. My kids were sad and I was, too. I guess sadness is contagious. My kids already know the way because we have been to São José dos Campos before.

. . . When we arrived in Rio I saw in the distance the ramshackle houses of the poor. I am afraid of those houses. To me they are a symbol of abject poverty. The passengers were getting up to grab their luggage. My suitcase was in the luggage compartment. I had given Cr$20 to the porter in São Paulo. As the bus was coming in I was looking around to see if I could see any reporters. When I saw them I perked up, smiled, and waved to them. They recognized me. They filmed my arrival. I greeted all those present. The reporters photographed me. Vera wanted to go to the hotel right away. After greeting everyone we went to the Serrador Hotel. What a magnificent building! We went to our room on the eleventh floor. It was a marvelous room. A snow-white bed and a fantastic view. Everything in Rio is beautiful. The housekeeper treated me well. Her name is Dona Luiza Fiori. She helped me put away our clothes and she said she was happy because she likes children.

Sr. Homero Homem, a learned poet, told me that we were going to be on a TV program. We ate, changed clothes, and left for the TV station. When we arrived the reporter asked about Audálio.

"He didn't come," Sr. Homero Homem replied.

The reporter got together with Sr. Homero Homem and decided to change the program, introducing me in a shack with my kids, Sr. Homero Homem, and Sr. Barboza Mello. We talked about the books I intend to write and the current one. They cited passages from the book.

We left the TV station, walked around some, and went to dine at the Churrascaria Gaúcha. Dona Luiza Fiori accompanied me. They rented a car and we went to the Serrador Hotel. How happy we were when we went to bed. The soft, snow-white bed!

November 8   I got up at four o'clock. I went to the window to get a view of the dazzling landscape of Rio de Janeiro. The little bread carts were circulating through the streets. Dona Luiza came up to ask me if I wanted to have breakfast.

She ordered coffee. The kids were astonished when they saw all the fruit and butter. Vera smiled when our eyes met. Now we are rich.

I took the elevator down to refill my pens. The hotel employees looked at the pens and smiled, remarking that the pens were old. I asked for a newspaper. I was in all of them. I spoke with the employees and then I took the elevator back up to read. I was tired but I was happy because life in Rio is like a dream. It's a fairyland. The Cariocas [natives of Rio de Janeiro] are really nice.

The hotel seems like an enchanted castle. It has everything we want. A radio, telephone, and a wonderful view. Dona Luiza Fiori is cultured and refined and also hard-working. I helped the kids change clothes and then we went to take a little tour of the city. The Cariocas were talking about my appearance on TV. I went to Cinelandia to see the places where I was going to sign books. I read the names of the publishing houses. We sat down and I read the *Ultima Hora*. I thought it was funny when I read, "A time clock for representatives in the National Congress." People recognized us. We walked along the streets looking for ink. The things that I need: books, ink, and paper. I found a store that sold pens and I asked if they had any ink. They said "yes." I asked the price: Cr$12. I counted my money and was Cr$5 short. The young man told me I could take the bottle of ink and pay him later. I was surprised because he didn't know me—that was the first time he had seen me. I told him I was staying at the Serrador Hotel.

"I trust you. You can take the ink."

. . . What fascinated me was the cultured ways of the hotel employees. They smiled when they saw me. It made me feel like I was in heaven. Dona Luiza told me I ought to take a bath. I took her advice. The famous writer Homero Homem came to the hotel and phoned my room. I asked him to come on up.

When Sr. Homero Homem came in he smiled and greeted us. He told me I should change before going to sign books at the offices of *Leitura* magazine. Dona Elza Heloisa was present. And also Dona Jurema Finamour. Phone calls started coming in from Cariocas who wanted to say hello. Sr. Homero Homem left. My kids were stunned. Vera looked at everything around her with amazement. What really impressed her was the bathroom. She said, "How can the water come out hot from behind the wall. Mama, is this an enchanted house like you read about in books?"

"It's not an enchanted house and it's not like the ones in those books. It's a hotel."

Dona Elza Heloisa left with my kids and I went to sign books at the editorial offices of *Leitura*. I was accompanied by Sr. Barboza Mello, who offered me a fruit drink. I liked it; it was the first time that I had had one. We ran up the steps. Sr. Homero Homem was seated and not wearing his jacket. He was writing. I let my eyes wander around the editorial offices. I was happy. I saw several books in the racks. I sat down to sign my books. A mulatto came up to me. He greeted me without giving his name. He asked Sr. Homero Homem if I could prove I was the author of the book. He said it in a subtle way. But I noticed.

"Yes," Sr. Homero Homem said in a calm voice.

The writer Walmir Ayala came in. He greeted me and looked me over closely. I felt like I was in front of a judge. Sr. Homero Homem introduced me, saying, "This is Walmir Ayala."

I thanked him for the article that he wrote about me in the *Jornal do Brasil* newspaper on September 1, 1960. I continued signing books. Sr. Barboza Mello kept asking me if I was tired. I told him I wasn't because now I don't get tired anymore. I'm not working. I remembered the times when I used to collect paper until eleven o'clock at night just to get money to buy something to eat.

November 9 I woke up at four because I was in the habit of getting up then. (. . .) The phone rang. I went to answer it and it was Dona Elza Heloisa. She said she was coming to take my kids for an outing. My room was packed with visitors. Dona Eva Vastari, a well-bred blonde woman from the Finnish magazine, was there. The phone rang. I went to answer it. It was Sr. Ferrão. I told him to come on up.

. . . The night was warm, the sky was starry. And the streets of Rio were overflowing with pedestrians. Sr. Ferrão accompanied me to Cinelandia, where the trees were lighted. When I arrived at the Book Fair the crowd applauded me. I waved and went over to the platform. I began my autographs with dedications. The plaza was overflowing. I was not able to be more attentive to the public because of my schedule. I had to go to the TV station. I hated to leave Cinelandia. The people holding on to me, asking me to sign books. We were able to get a taxi. I was tired of being on my feet. We went to eat dinner. At the restaurant we selected what we wanted to eat. I was horrified because the women were throwing out half of the food. And at the price of food these days!

It's just that I'm in the habit of eating everything, so I don't know how to waste food.

What a magnificent restaurant! The waiters were attentive, staring at me curiously when someone called out my name.

November 10   Sr. Homero Homem phoned me and said he would pick me up to go sign books. Dona Elza Heloisa told me she would take me. I noticed that the streets of Rio were just as congested as São Paulo's. The hurly-burly. Dona Elza Heloisa and I walked swiftly. Dona Luiza Fiori went to the movies with my kids. What I really admire about the Cariocas is their solidarity. A united and sociable people. Sr. Homero Homem and Sr. Barboza Mello were at the editorial offices of *Leitura*. I greeted them and sat down to sign my books.

I told Sr. Homero Homem that I liked him and I was willing to buy him on the installment plan. He told me, "I only sell myself on a cash basis."

Sr. Walmir Ayala left abruptly without saying goodbye. Sr. Barboza Mello was kind and considerate. Sr. Homero told me, "You know, Carolina, I'm a fisherman. I'm going to write a book like yours. I'm going to buy a boat and we'll go sailing. Every Friday I'm going fishing."

Sr. Barboza Mello asked me if I was tired. He really doesn't know anything about my life. I don't tire easily. I went to change clothes because I was going to sign books in the plaza. When I got to the hotel I met Sr. Raimundo Bevilaqua. He told me he wanted to marry me. I thought it was funny.

. . . When I got to the square to sign books, a huge crowd was there waiting for me. I signed books and told the Cariocas a few

anecdotes. (. . .) A young man came up and asked me to autograph a 5-cruzeiro bill for him.

"I can't sign the bill."

"It's because I can't afford to buy the book."

Senhor Ferrão gave him a book and I signed it. The young
man smiled when he received it. He smiled with contentment as if
he had just received a present worth a lot of money.

Dona Jurema Finamour and Dona Luiza were at my side. I was
going to be interviewed on TV at 10 P.M. We went by car to Urca.

. . . When we left the TV station Dona Jurema Finamour's
husband took me to the hotel. I went to bed thinking that I should
get up early because I had made plans with Diva—she was going to
pick me up in the morning so I could attend the mass said by the
bishop, Dom Helder Camara.

November 11 I got up at five o'clock. I got ready and went down the
elevator. I met Dona Diva and her sister, who is a teacher. She
drove the car. She got her streets mixed up and was a bad driver.
. . . When we got to the Ana Nery Nursing School, Dom Helder
was celebrating mass. I was horrified with the way the sanctuary
looked—there was nobody there. I counted eleven people inside
the church. Dom Helder says the entire mass with such joy—it is an
impressive sight.

When he left the altar I went into the visitation room. Dona
Diva introduced me to him. He is a little man. I told him that I
have been following his philanthropic works. He began to speak,
"We have to improve the situation the world is in. When I look at
the world I see that we have great social reforms to carry out. It
is not possible for one third of humanity to have everything and
two thirds not to have anything. (. . .) We have to be good so as to
multiply our examples. I love the rich as well as the poor. Because
the rich are of God and the poor are of God."

He commented on some passages from my book. We said
goodbye and returned.

. . . When I got back to the hotel I met the reporters from the
magazine who were there to interview me. Two women came to
visit me. We began to talk. My room was adorned with beautiful

flowers that the Cariocas had sent me. A fat woman, a loudmouth, was there showing off her talents. She was a composer and a writer. She wouldn't allow the reporter to interview me. He was nervous and we went to another place to finish the interview. I went into the other room. He was cursing and saying how he couldn't tolerate a woman that was a chatterbox. I thought I would be indirect. . . . He interviewed me and promised to give me a book—*The Little Prince.*

Dona Jurema Finamour came in and we began to talk. The reporters from the magazine *Manchete* arrived and invited me to visit the favelas. We went to the Mangue favela. I was not received very well by the residents. (. . .) I walked along the beaches and saw the Cariocas in their bathing suits, lying on the sand, as carefree as the birds that roam the wide-open spaces.

We headed for the hotel. Dona Luiza Fiori was waiting for us for lunch. Dona Helena Figueiredo arrived. She invited me to go out with her; she was going to take my picture for a story. We hired a taxi. She photographed me in the doorway of the Brazilian Academy of Letters. The door was closed.

I seated Vera and José Carlos near the bust of Machado de Assis [Brazilian novelist and short story writer, 1839–1908].

. . . I was tired. My feet were swollen and they hurt. We got in a car and went to take the bus to São Paulo.

November 12   Dr. Lélio told me I should go to the TV station. (. . .) Carlos Felipe Moysés accompanied me. We arrived at TV Tupi at 11:30 A.M. When we sat down at the table I counted eighteen people. Sr. Mauricio Loureiro Gama [and the boxer] Primo Carnera next to me and the singer Carmelia Alves. We started eating lunch. Primo Carnera complained that there wasn't enough to eat. I was shocked when I saw the size of Primo Carnera's hands and feet. Sr. Mauricio Loureiro Gama wanted me to ask Primo Carnera if he wanted to fight "Tico-Tico," the boxer José Carlos de Moraes.

. . . I went to talk to the reporter in order to arrange for our trip to Rio. We were going to a party at the Renaissance Club. The reporter said I should be at the editorial offices at nine o'clock to take the plane.

November 13 . . . We took a car and headed for the airport. We met some reporter friends. They asked me if I like to fly. It was raining when we boarded the plane. My heart was pounding in my chest when we took off. The reporter sat next to me chatting and reading the newspapers. The plane was overtaking the rain clouds. The whirling clouds were coming up to meet the plane. They are white like balls of cotton. I was praying, asking God to help us arrive without incident.

When we arrived in Rio I saw familiar faces waiting for me. The writer Homero Homem; Sr. Oscar, manager of the Renaissance Club; Sr. Barboza Mello; the poet Raimundo Bevilaqua; and the reporters that were photographing us. They didn't know Audálio. We went to the home of Sr. Oscar, who is a lawyer. What a magnificent house! Several blacks greeted me.

. . . I was hungry, Dr. Oscar's wife offered me feijoada [rice, beans, and meat]. I took a bath, ironed my dress, and we went to the Renaissance Club. A black who is a lawyer spoke to me about how hard it was to study. He told me he was a bricklayer's assistant. He studied at night.

. . . At the Renaissance Club the party was lively. The blacks of Rio were well dressed. The reporters were present. The festivities began with a fashion show, as a competition. Four models were judged. A speech was given and reference was made to my being in attendance. I was applauded.

. . . I said goodbye to Dr. Oscar and his wife and we left with the reporter Darwin Brandão and his wife. We went to Copacabana to have dinner. The writer Homero Homem accompanied us. I took notice of the refined manners of Sr. Darwin Brandão. As a driver he observes the traffic signals.

After dinner he drove us to Dr. Oscar's residence. It was 2 A.M.

November 14 . . . After breakfast Dr. Oscar drove us to the airport. When we got on the plane the reporter saw Dona Sarita Campos and greeted her.

"Who is that woman?"

"It's Sarita Campos."

I sat down next to Dona Sarita Campos. She was holding a
rosary and was praying. (. . .) When we arrived in São Paulo, Dona
Sarita perked up. We said our goodbyes.

. . . I went to see my kids and get them dressed because we
were going to visit the mayor, Adhemar de Barros. (. . .) In the
waiting room several people were waiting their turn to see him. A
TV crew was also waiting. When Dr. Adhemar came out to receive
me I walked in his direction and greeted him and recited a few
verses. He told me he was going to organize a commission to build
houses for the people in the favelas.

November 17   . . . I was going to go out for an evening of book
signings organized by the columnist Alik Kostakis. I had on my
red coat. (. . .) We took a taxi and went to the Conjunto Nacional
on the Avenida Paulista. The books were a benefit for the São
Francisco Childrens' Home. The stalls were decorated with
flowers of different hues. My stall was in the back part of the
room. The elegant, well-dressed ladies of São Paulo arrived. My
patroness was Dona Bia Coutinho. I was seeing her for the first
time. She treated me exceptionally well. She didn't give me her
address, and she didn't invite me to her house.

. . . The most cheerful one there was Count Ermelindo
Matarazzo. Writers and artists were present. The writers went
to my stall: Dona Adalgisa Nery, Dona Maria Dezone Pacheco
Fernandes, Mattos Pacheco, Sr. José Tavares de Miranda.

. . . I was horrified listening to a high-society woman say that
she was happy when her husband died. I feel like I am living in a
world of fake jewelry.

November 18   . . . I am going to São José do Rio Pardo. Vera was
excited. We went on the bus. I contemplated our country's
exuberance and the vast stretches of uncultivated land. I don't
blame the country people for abandoning the lands because
they work hard and never have anything. I, too, had left the
countryside. (. . .) Once again I saw the rural landscapes and
contemplated the flight of the birds in the vast open spaces. When
we arrived in São José do Rio Pardo, Sr. Thercio Gonçalves was

waiting for us. A cultured and likable fellow. President of the Euclydes da Cunha Student Union. What I noticed in the city: everybody admires and respects Euclydes da Cunha [Brazilian writer, 1866–1909].

. . . It was warm in the city. The inhabitants were calm. So different from the people of São Paulo, who seem so agitated and clumsy when you see them walking along the street. The resident of São Paulo pushes anybody that happens to be in front of him and steps on the feet of those next to him. We stayed in a charming old building. (. . .) The receptions were very nice.

What really impressed me was the food served in the hotel. What a delicious meal! I was happy, calm, and content. I was smiling all the time. It seemed like I was in another world. A sublime world, one without confusions. (. . .) We spent Sunday in São José do Rio Pardo. Dr. Osvaldo Gallotti drove us around so we could see the sights. I saw the shack where Euclydes da Cunha wrote *Os Sertões* [*Rebellion in the Backlands*].

. . . Dr. Osvaldo Gallotti and Sr. Thercio Gonçalves took us to the city's hydroelectric plant, which supplies energy for neighboring cities all the way to Mooca. (. . .) I admired the great number of mango trees scattered over the plains. What a magnificent day! The birds were flying around overhead. It was a sight that the residents of São Paulo can't appreciate. The birds seem to be afraid of the skies over São Paulo because of the smoke from the factories.

. . . We went to the underground level to see where the electricity is generated. The tunnel looks like a cave.

We went to see Dr. Gallotti's mother. Her house is huge. It is just the right size for the holidays when her grandchildren come to visit. I took a tour of the house. What a big house! And it has such old furniture. When I was a young girl I dreamed of being the owner of a mansion with several wings.

. . . We went to the orphanage to see the children in the care of the Sisters. Those children looked sad. They must dream of being free, but they are happier than the ones that roam the streets without a roof over their heads. They sang the song "Criança Feliz" ["Happy Child"]. Vera said to me, "I am happier than they are because I have a mother."

And she looked at me tenderly.

. . . Sunday passed uneventfully. It was a really short day. Days are long in the favela: hunger, fighting, and police cars. I was happy with the present that Sr. Thercio Gonçalves gave me—a book. The book was *Os Sertões.*

My thanks go out to the people of São José do Rio Pardo. I was treated really well. The warm reception that the people gave me has encouraged me to study and to write other books.

We traveled that night. I was singing during the trip. Life is great! I've got a cushy life. Now I have food, a house, and clothes to wear. I buy myself new clothes. When I used to dig around in the garbage cans looking for clothes to wear I would think: some day I'm going to buy clothes for myself. And God helped me. I'm happy.

November 23   I am a little uneasy about writing a diary about my current life. Writing critically about the rich people. They are powerful and they can destroy me. There are some who ask me for money and beg me not to mention them. There is a woman who wants money to buy a house. I don't have it. She got upset with me. She wants Cr$500,000.

I haven't been writing lately. I'm thinking, thinking, thinking. When I criticized the slum dwellers in my diary they threw rocks at me . . .

. . . Every day I get letters from foreign publishers that want to translate my book. I am really shocked by the repercussions the book has had.

November 24   My kids are happy because they can buy fruit to eat. And they used to go through the garbage cans. José Carlos says, "It seems like we're dreaming. There are so many things to eat, but you have to have money to buy things. Who invented money?"

"It was a race of people called Phoenicians."

"It was a really stupid invention, wasn't it, Mama?"

I am thinking about where I am going to leave Vera when I travel. I had not counted on so much traveling. I went into the city. Dr. Lélio told me he had already sent books to Porto Alegre. I saw Dona Elza Heloisa. She told me she is going to accompany me on the trip to Porto Alegre. I bought stockings and dresses. When I reached Osasco I found José Carlos complaining that Sr. Antonio Soeiro Cabral had spanked him. José Carlos sounds intelligent when he speaks, but he plays a lot of pranks.

November 26   My kids are confused by the sudden changes that have come about in our lives. They buy apples, smile, and remark, "It's great to be able to buy whatever you want."

Vera asked, "Are we always going to live this way?"

"I'm in the cinder-block house now."

"Do you remember when it flooded in the favela? Water came in the house. Poor Nenê. Poor Ivanice. It's terrible for a little girl to live in the favela."

The book seller Paulo Rolim de Moura came complaining that City Hall wanted to close down his bookstore in Penha. He asked me to go talk to a politician and get them to leave him alone. (. . .) I told him I don't have any influence with politicians because I don't butter them up.

"Please, Dona Carolina. You can do anything, even the sun gives in to your wishes."

I smiled thinking what he said was funny. Who am I? A hummingbird talking to an eagle. I got tired of explaining to him how useless it would be for me to interfere. He went away sad and depressed.

November 30   I got up at four to get us ready to go to Porto Alegre. I asked Dona Maria to take care of the house, wash the clothes, and keep an eye on the kids. They get into a lot of mischief and the neighbors complain and advise me to have them placed in a children's home. Now that I'm able to put food on the table I should send them away? That would be an unjust thing for me to do.

. . . I put on my red coat and took a taxi. I had the driver stop where people were waiting to get the bus and offered to take someone into town. Some of them refused my offer, thinking that they would have to pay the fare. They were right to be cautious because workers' salaries can be compared to an eyedropper. A little woman of Portuguese descent who works in the Jardim America district accepted my invitation. I kept up my conversation with the driver. I was happy. I was getting to know Brazil.

When I reached the airport the porters came out to meet me saying, "Look, it's my girlfriend!"

It was seven o'clock and the sky was cold and gray.

"Where are you going?"

"To Porto Alegre."

I kept moving around, constantly looking at the clock and thinking about Dona Elza Heloisa. What if she doesn't show up? I don't know how to travel by myself. The people that were arriving recognized me. At eight o'clock Dona Elza arrived and went to take care of the tickets. A woman asked me, "Is that woman your personal assistant?"

"She is a journalist who is accompanying me to Porto Alegre. I am not used to traveling by myself. I used to live in the favela. And the slum dweller's itinerary consists of the hospital, police headquarters, and the investigation room.

. . . When the plane took off I was calm, sitting next to Dona Elza Heloisa. She was telling me that she lived in Porto Alegre. (. . .) I was contemplating the majestic landscape and the huge tracts of uncultivated land. I was thinking: so much abandoned land and the common folk are starving! Those lands belong to the capitalists. No one can occupy the land and cultivate it without their consent. They have the money to buy off the Law and its entanglements. For the world to become a good place the lands have to be free. Man can gather what the land yields because it is inexhaustible. If the lands are free, everybody can plant and poverty will vanish. Well-fed people are happy people. (. . .) Why doesn't the government redistribute the lands among the common folk?

I think about this but I don't say anything because if I say it the capitalists will say, "Carolina is a Red. She is ignorant and semiliterate."

As the plane was following its course the view was changing. It was becoming transformed. Some unforgettable places. There are those who have money who say they are going to Europe, instead of getting to know the happy places in our own country.

In Porto Alegre, Sr. Assis Marques, the distributor for books published by Francisco Alves, was with photographers and reporters awaiting my arrival.

. . . We went to eat lunch. What a delicious meal. What excellent meat. Sitting there in that fashionable restaurant, I thought about those unfortunate ones who pick up what's left over from the markets in order to eat. I feel like those unfortunate souls that go hungry are my children. I came out of the favela. I feel like I emerged from the sea and left my brothers to drown.

After lunch we went to the radio station. The local people gave me curious looks. Sr. Assis said we were going to Pelotas. We went by car. Sr. Assis's wife accompanied us. We left at 5 A.M. So much land! I was contemplating the golden wheat fields. There is more agriculture in Rio Grande do Sul. Looking at the farmers at their tasks I remembered my childhood. How beautiful the world is now!

When we arrived in Pelotas I looked around as if I were waking from a dream. I recalled the cities I had read about in geography class and my teacher from long ago explaining to me, "Pelotas is the sweet city. It has a candy factory."

And I thought, What can the word "factory" mean? My dream was to have a dictionary, because [my childhood teacher] Dona Lanita told me that I could learn many things by reading a dictionary.

My life is in a spin. Several people were waiting for me. Among them was Dr. João Carlos Gastal, the mayor. We went to the hotel. What a calm city. The people were calmly going about their business. At two o'clock we went to have lunch. My blood pressure was normal again. I was happy.

The radio station broadcast my interview. The mayor heard it on his portable radio. There were twenty-five of us at the table. I was seated next to the mayor. I thought, On another occasion I was sitting in the police car and now I was next to the mayor. Dona Heloisa, the mayor's wife, said, "What I admire is the fact that

Carolina comes from the favela and she knows how to eat with a knife and fork."

I laughed heartily. Looking at the snow-white tables decorated with flowers in vases, I thought, I am living in a historic moment. This is a palace. This is a paradise.

. . . I went to autograph books at the Book Fair in the plaza. Several people were waiting for me. I heard a young man say, "What an ugly black woman!"

I smiled and told him, "I think drunks and lazy people are ugly."

I signed books with great affection. I wanted to look at the plaza so I could describe it, but I couldn't because of the huge number of books to be signed. All I saw was a grove of bottle-green trees and a few little book stalls scattered here and there. I thought the plaza was all decked out. It had books. A little black fellow who was walking around said in a voice loud enough for all to hear, "You know, Carolina, I wish you would include in your diary that there is racial prejudice here in the South."

The white people that were present exchanged looks, thinking that the black man's complaints were inappropriate. I stopped so I could hear him. I believe I ought to take into consideration my colored brothers.

"Okay. I will include your accusation in my diary."

Does that mean that there is racial prejudice in southern Brazil? Could the Brazilian southerners be imitating the people in the United States? The little black fellow said goodbye and left happy as if he had accomplished a great feat. I thought: he trusts me and knows that I am going to include him in my diary. I am going to register his complaint.

. . . I bought a book: *Doces de Pelotas* [Candy from Pelotas]. The woman who wrote it signed it for me. I paid Cr$150 for the book. She wrote the following dedication in it: "To Carolina Maria de Jesus, the phenomenon of the century. With great admiration from a modest confectioner from Princesa do Sul. 11/30/1960—Maria Collares Polavera."

When the autograph session was over, we went to the radio station and then to the club. Fica Aí—a club for blacks. What an elegant club. It has a large ballroom with a place for the orchestra. The mayor was there with his wife, tasting the candy with great delight. When the blacks complained about racial segregation, the mayor became silent. His lips shut down like the hands of a clock when they stop. I thought: this man knows how to live. He would not be displeasing to Pilate or Caesar.

After the eating and the drinking the blacks gave their speeches. A strange speech. Racial grumblings. I thought, How long will this quarrel go on between blacks and whites? There is so much living space in the world. Man is not eternal. In his earthly sojourn he should try to live in peace. Man has the obligation to direct his thinking toward good. The beautiful and the pure. And not harbor ill will toward his fellow man.

When it was my turn to speak, I expressed gratitude for the tributes I had received. (. . .) I was given a memento from the Fica Aí Club. A silver book with the inscription, "Only books can immortalize a people. To Carolina Maria de Jesus, Fica-Aí Cultural Club. Pelotas, 11/30/60."

. . . The return trip was delightful. I saw the farms again. I saw a pretty house. They had planted a rose bush and the stalks had wrapped around the walls. It was in bloom. I would like to live in that house.

When we arrived in Porto Alegre, the Guaiba River bridge was being raised to let a ship sail through. It was a beautiful spectacle.

December 1 . . . In the afternoon I went to sign books at the Globo Bookstore. I was already familiar with the building from photographs. The people were sad and agitated over the bread shortage. The bakers were on strike, trying to get a price increase. (. . .) While I was signing I didn't let them form a line. I wanted to be in the middle of the people.

. . . I visited the mayor, Sr. Loureiro da Silva. He mentioned that he visits the favelas because he was elected by the slum dwellers. He had schools built and nine kilometers of waterpipes laid. He built the Art Center. He told me to ask the inhabitants of the favelas for information about his administration.

That evening I visited the TV station. I thanked the citizens of

Porto Alegre and the people of Pelotas. I went to the theater. I attended the play "The Farce of the Perfect Wife," by Dona Edy Lima. I had met Dona Edy Lima at the airport. (. . .) I gave thanks to God when I went to bed. I was tired. We were going to return the next day.

December 2 We got up at four and packed our bags. Sr. Assis arrived at 7:00 informing us that the governor had requested that I remain in the state one more day. So that I could go visit the favelas. I went to buy newspapers. I went out with Sr. Assis. I was happy when I arrived at the governor's mansion. I saw several colored servants. The maid led me into the room where I was to speak with Dona Neuza Brizola. I sat down and noticed the furnishings. When Dona Neuza Goulart Brizola came in I watched her attentively. She was the first governor's wife to receive me after I left the favela. In talking to Dona Neuza I observed that the majestic palace in which she lived had not made her haughty. I thought it was nice when she said, "Carolina, this mansion hasn't made me vain. I am afraid of this house. My husband is a politician. And politicians don't have any friends."

. . . She said goodbye and I went to talk to Dr. Leonel Brizola in another room. I asked him about the state's development. (. . .) Dr. Leonel Brizola asked me not to become proud and haughty and not to look down on the poor people.

"You ought to return periodically to the favela so you don't lose your authenticity. You will visit the favelas of Porto Alegre and tell the people there that they need to and ought to study. Do me that favor. My dream is to eradicate illiteracy in the state. My car is at your disposal."

I laughed loudly and remarked, "What an honor for me. The only times I used to ride around, it was in a police car."

Sr. Assis and I said goodbye to Dr. Leonel Brizola. What a fine car! The cushions are like silk. I waited in the hotel for a visit from Dona Neuza Brizola's secretary, who was going to accompany me to the favelas. (. . .) At three o'clock the secretary arrived with her husband. We drove through the poor districts of Porto Alegre. I was shocked when I saw the favelas of Rio Grande do Sul.

The houses are well-built units made of wooden boards. They have plenty of water and several reservoirs. The women don't fight over the water. (. . .) Some of the people in the favela knew me by name. I saw a large room with armchairs and a blackboard, where the children study. The ones who teach the children are the nuns and priests.

. . . When the people crowded together I gave the speech asking the people to study. Knowing how to read is a good thing and it makes life more enjoyable. A little girl who was paying close attention to my words asked, "Mama, is this black woman crazy? Do you think she might have escaped from the asylum?"

In fact, the asylum is close to the favela. I let out a big laugh. I was happy. (. . .) The favela is at the top of a hill. To get there we went by station wagon. The place where the favela is located is beautiful. From there, you can see the entire city. The place is dry. A man who was accompanying us said, "These poor people of Rio Grande do Sul are rich. The poor people are those that live in the favelas of São Paulo and Rio and in the North."

What really impressed me about the favela of Porto Alegre was the amount of water available. When you turn on the faucet, within two minutes you can fill up your container. The women wash clothes with running water disinfected with chlorine.

. . . We returned to Porto Alegre. I was happy. The second favela I visited was Vila Vargas, known as Coreia. (. . .) In all the favelas I visited I said, "You all ought to learn to read."

One woman asked me, "Do you feel okay being away from the favela?"

"I feel better. The favela is a garbage dump and my dream is to live in a cinder-block house. If I didn't know how to read, I would have to live in the favela for the remainder of my life."

. . . An old black woman gave me a little bunch of flowers. I thanked her and kissed the flowers. There wasn't enough time to visit all the favelas; they are scattered. I said goodbye to Dona Neuza Brizola's assistant.

. . . Thursday night we had a reception at the Galeto Sherezade Restaurant. A combined tribute given by the Press Association of Rio Grande do Sul and Yazigi Language Institute; they had a banquet in our honor.

. . . We went to the State House Chamber to witness the Second State Congress of Aldermen. It was exciting. Governor Brizola was there. I said to him, "You are following me. . . ."

He smiled and said, "No, Carolina. You are the one who is chasing after me. I got here first."

. . . The presiding official interrupted the debates to receive me. He introduced me to those present, inviting me to take part in the debates. He asked me what causes favelas to spring up in the big cities. I answered, "Those of us who live in the favela are country people. Because the land owners continue exploiting us unchecked we have left the big farms and moved to the city. And in the big cities the ones that have a good life are those who are educated. Those of us without any education encounter hardships in life. Even if we have a job in the city as a salaried employee, we face hardships because our wages aren't enough to pay our bills. It's not possible to pay for decent housing. We have to occupy public land."

I managed to write some verses and publish them in several newspapers. My observations on the farm worker and the land owner:

> The Brazilian says
> that slavery has ended.
> The farm worker sweats all year long
> and never has a dime.
>
> If the laborer is sick
> he still has to work.
> The poor man struggles in the hot sun
> and he doesn't have anything to show for it.
>
> At five in the morning
> the foreman plays reveille
> waking up the worker
> to go harvest the crops.
>
> He arrives in the field as the sun comes up
> each one in his row
> sweating, and to eat
> he has only black beans and corn meal.

He will never see his gloomy situation
get any better
he doesn't buy meat
to avoid getting into debt to the boss.

At the end of the month the land owner
gives him a voucher for 100,000 *réis* [old unit of currency]
something that costs six
he sells to the worker for ten.

The peasant doesn't have a future
and he works all day long
the poor fellow has no insurance
and no retirement pension.

He loses his youth
his whole life in the countryside
and he doesn't belong to an organization
where is his union?

He spends the whole year
working—what a feat!
the farm owner gets rich
and he winds up in poverty.

If the farm owner were to speak:
"Don't stay on my farm."
The peasant has to move
since there's no one to defend him.

They applauded me. I glanced at Dr. Leonel Brizola. He was
smiling. (. . .) I signed some books for the aldermen.
. . . If only I could visit all the states of Brazil! I was happy. I
thought, This is a dream! I used to walk along Tiradentes Avenue
in São Paulo digging around in the trash cans. Crying with
hunger. And today . . . I am in the presence of the most
prominent figures in the country.
I have read the stories of the fairies that transformed
unfortunate souls into princes and princesses. I used to say,
Happiness has turned its back on me. Now it has grabbed me by
the arms. (. . .) When I left the legislative chamber I received a

blue banner with the inscription, "Second State Congress of Aldermen—December 1–3, 1960—Porto Alegre—Rio Grande do Sul."

I got back to the hotel and started packing my bags for the return trip.

December 3   I got up at six and went to buy newspapers to take back to São Paulo. I went into a bar to have a cup of coffee. I bought the *Diário de Notícias.* The people there wanted autographs and I accommodated them, all the while fearing that I would miss the plane.

. . . We left Porto Alegre at eight o'clock. The sky was blue and the plane didn't vibrate. I saw those flat lands, farm land. I was able to distinguish the wheat fields by the yellow gold color. (. . .) It was a direct flight to São Paulo.

. . . Today we are going to Rio at 3 P.M. (. . .) When we got to the airport the porters asked me, "Where are you going this time? Who pays for your flights?

"The rich magazines. *Leitura, Time, Life,* and *O Cruzeiro.*"

One of the porters smiled and said, "Yes . . . I'm going to write a diary."

Audálio was already at the airport. It was Saturday. My kids were happy. They said, "We are going to the Serrador Hotel. I'm going to take a bath in the big tub! We are rich now and we can go by plane."

At three the plane took off. The kids were singing. At four o'clock we were in Rio. We felt like we had just jumped from São Paulo to Rio. David St. Clair was at the airport. (. . .) He came to meet us accompanied by a woman photographer. After exchanging greetings David St. Clair had me photographed as I got my luggage.

(. . .) We took a taxi that went through the streets of downtown Rio. We went to the Copacabana Palace [Hotel]. I was well received by the proprietor of the hotel. David St. Clair was in a happy mood, trying to get the photographer to take a picture of me in front of the mirror. He asked, "Carolina, do you like this room?"

My kids were restless. They thought the room was too

confining because they were moving around a lot and the
furniture was always getting in their way. (. . .) David St. Clair
was very thoughtful and considerate. He told me that he would
arrange for someone to take care of my kids. They ordered
dinner. The kids were getting into mischief in the bathroom. I
felt like slapping José Carlos, but I didn't want to make a scene in
the hotel. For dinner they brought risotto made with chicken and
milk. The kids didn't like it. Now that we've left the favela the kids
have become picky about what they eat.

. . . I called the housekeeper and asked if I could get a dress
washed right away.

"No, only on Monday. The laundry is closed. Where are you
from?"

"I am from the favela."

"The favela?" she asked quizzically, changing her voice,
shaking her head and looking at me with repugnance as she
repeated, "from the favela to the hotel, to the hotel!"

By the way she talked I could tell that she was a foreigner. She
left, saying that she would not be able to wait on me. When she left
I cursed her, "Mary Stuart dethroned!"

The woman who was going to watch the kids arrived and
demanded that they should go to sleep.

. . . I went out wearing my pea-print dress. We went to eat
at the Bon Gourmet Restaurant. What luxury! I saw several women
displaying their expensive jewelry, drinking champagne and
wine. They were looking at the menu, choosing with indifference
what they were going to eat. You got the impression they weren't
hungry. They are rich and from the time they were kids they have
heard, "Eat, daughter! Eat, son!"

. . . Several women came over to talk to me about poverty,
telling me I ought to resolve the problem of the inhuman
conditions in which the country's slum dwellers live. I presented
the facts. The task of solving the problem falls to those in the
middle class and above, the ones who dominate the country. . . .
I wasn't familiar with the menu. The reporter told me what was
on it. I ordered asparagus soup and creme suzette.

I swallowed that strange dish and was still hungry.

One gentleman told me that he was going to make a donation to the slum dwellers. I noticed that they wanted to impress the American reporters and the photographers that were taking pictures of us. They prepared my meal at the table. My table was the only one that had flowers on it, red roses. I like roses. In the bouquet of roses there was a card with an inscription: *Life.* At the next table there was a reporter observing us. I was calm because I was sitting next to Audálio, my friend and protector. (. . .) When I started to get irritated with those nocturnal butterflies that I hated, he said, "Don't get all worked up. Write about it. Put your reactions in your diary."

David St. Clair didn't say anything. He just listened. He was staring at me. (. . .) I was eager to leave that restaurant. It seemed like those ladies just wanted to show off their fancy attire, each one trying to be more chic than the next. I saw a tall slender black man who looked like a swordfish circulating in that part of the room. He had a stately manner.

"That's the singer."

. . . We went by car to the Night and Day. When we arrived all the tables were taken. The minute I entered the place people recognized me. I sat down at a small table with my protectors: Audálio and David St. Clair. He went to tell Grande Othello [a famous black actor] to introduce me on the stage. After Othello had greeted me the curiosity of those around me doubled. Some came to my table. (. . .) The women who were at my table spoke about social reform.

"It is not right for us to leave the slum dwellers relegated to the garbage dump. You did a service in alerting us to the problem. We have to protect those who are less fortunate. You display great courage in fighting to escape from that hole."

I thought, They are philanthropists in word only. They talk big, but it's just talk. Chattering parrots. It's only when they see me that they remember there are favelas in Brazil.

. . . We took a taxi and went to the Copacabana Palace Hotel. When we got to the hotel the kids were sleeping. The sitter that was with them left saying, "I swear! Those kids are like bats out of hell."

I went to bed. I couldn't fall asleep because of the heat. I thanked God when it was daybreak and the kids woke up. José Carlos wanted to jump out the window. He said, "I'll jump and land in the swimming pool."

"Don't do that, José Carlos," I warned him when he started leaning out the window.

December 4 . . . The kids didn't have anything to wear. Just dirty clothes. The housekeeper came at eight o'clock. She looked around the room and said, "Don't let your children touch the mirror."

Because she looked foreign, I asked her, "What country are you from?"

"I am from Vienna."

"Ah, the waltz capital!"

I began to hum the "Blue Danube." She smiled and invited me to dance. She looked at the room, noticing how my clothes were lying around all over the place, and asked me, "Do you have a personal assistant?"

"An assistant? . . . I am a former slum dweller and people who live in the favela don't have anything."

"What do you do?"

"I am going to study a little bit more and I want to be a writer."

"You can't study and write with these kids hanging around you. Be careful with the mirrors! Don't leave the faucet running!"

I thought, My God, with so many instructions I'm going to go crazy. I'm going to walk back to São Paulo. I started to pack my clothes in the suitcase. I got the kids dressed and ready to go and left the hotel.

. . . I stopped a car and asked the driver to take me to the Serrador Hotel. I began to complain about my life. If I had known that things in my life would become so confused I would have stayed in the favela and I would still be picking up paper.

. . . I had my picture taken by the swimming pool. The hotel guests were looking at me and saying, "Look at Carolina. She's gotten rich."

Some people came to talk to David St. Clair. As they approached they were looking at me. I don't know Rio well enough to mention all the places we went. We got on a boat and went sailing. Paulo Muniz photographed me.

December 5 . . . At nine David St. Clair phoned for me to come down with my suitcases. (. . .) David St. Clair took me to a store in the Copacabana district to buy some dresses and have me photographed trying them on. After that, we went to a jewelry store. He introduced me to the store owners and said, "They are Americans."

They spoke English and the only thing I understood was the "Garbage Room" [*Quarto de Despejo*]. I started to sweat. I realized that a black person becomes a little uneasy in the presence of a North American. It seems like they look at blacks with repugnance. How blacks must suffer in the United States. I felt afraid, and then I thought, My God, I'm in Brazil. I'm a Brazilian citizen. Here whites vote, and blacks vote, too. Here in my Brazil blacks dance the *quadrilha* face to face with whites. (. . .) My kids were misbehaving and I came back to reality. [These people] were doing a story for the newspaper.

When they had finished, we got in a taxi and went to the airport. (. . .) The taxi was going along and I was singing [my samba] "Ra Re Ri Ro Rua."[30] David St. Clair said, "Carolina, you could sing in a night club."

People at the Santos Dumont Airport recognized me, saying, "I enjoyed your book."

Books were available at the airport. The passengers bought them and asked me to autograph them. They remarked, "The people that live in the slums of São Paulo suffer more than Rio's slum dwellers."

. . . We got on the plane. At 1:00 P.M. we were in São Paulo. We got in a car and went to Osasco. The neighbors were talking about my constant traveling. I'm not the one that pays for the trips. The house was dirty and full of fleas. I bought a liter of bug poison to kill the fleas. I was tired. I went to bed and fell asleep. I woke up thinking about David St. Clair and all the confusion in the hotel. I thought I could still hear the hotel maid criticizing my children. My kids were accustomed to the mud. They used to live in garbage. They didn't know the comforts of the rich. They think where we are now is fabulous and unbelievable. To slum dwellers cinder-block houses are fairy-tale palaces. All slum dwellers dream of living in a cinder-block house. Everybody has their ideal.

An ideal is the clothing of the soul.

December 6 I was happy and felt reinvigorated. It was a beautiful day and I was singing. (. . .) I changed clothes and went downtown. When I go by a bookstore, the store owners invite me to come in and sign books. They see me smiling and remark what a lucky person I am. With all the outward displays directed toward me I am a little uneasy on the inside. I feel like I am really just iron covered with a layer of gold. And one day the gold leaf is going to fade and I will return to my natural state—iron.

. . . The reporter told me that he is looking for a house for me to buy. I was happy inside and out. And I smiled. My dream was beginning to take shape. I am going to have a cinder-block house with several rooms in it and other little structures next to the house. A room to take a bath in. Just imagine that—me taking a bath in a bathtub. I, who have led such a primitive life, bathing in a tub. I received some publicity shots when my book was released and I am going to have them framed to adorn my cinder-block house. (. . .) We agreed that tomorrow I would go to town to look for a house. I'm in a hurry to do it. It feels like I am dreaming. I am going to buy a cinder-block house of my own. To a slum dweller a house is so important that the word ought to be written in capital letters—CINDER-BLOCK HOUSE.

December 7 . . . I left the kids at home and went downtown. People give me curious looks. Some of them congratulate me, others attack me saying that my book is getting people stirred up. I explain things by saying that the favela exists and the number of slum dwellers is doubling along with the cost of living. I went to the editorial offices. (. . .) I saw some houses in the Cantareira district. They were too old and too big. They had some rooms that could be rented, but I don't want to live with other tenants.

The reporter took me to 562 Benta Pereira Street. It was hard for us to find the street. I don't like two-story houses because it's like there are two houses. I like a house with two entrances. The reporter liked the house, and so I ought to like it, too. For a slum dweller just anything will suffice. Even though I am a slum dweller with the tastes of King Solomon. The house is on top of a hill, it has a front yard and a window with an iron grating. The window is as big as the room. It has a plastic curtain with colorful roses printed on it. José Carlos got out of the car and went in to see the inside of the house. It has two bedrooms and several beds. A woman who had dirty-looking skin accompanied us. She said that the house was for sale. (. . .) The reporter liked the living room. It's big and should be divided with a curtain. When we left the house we drove to the real estate agency that has the house listed. The one who waited on us was Sr. João, one of the partners in the firm. The reporter said that I could buy the house and pay for it. The price is Cr$1,550,000. I was worried about the high price. Just trust God, I thought. It looks like favorable winds are protecting me. It's just that I am afraid to buy anything. When I left the real estate agency I left happy. The agent said the house was empty. That the people living there were being taken care of by Sr. Carivaldo, the owner of the house.

We went to the bookstore. I told Dr. Lélio that I was going to buy a cinder-block house.

December 8 Today is a holiday. I'm not going to leave the house. I'm not going to write in my diary because I'm afraid to refer to the turmoil in the lives of the people in the "living room." They are ambitious and they remark with a dose of resentment, "Carolina's rich."

December 9 I got up at six o'clock. Today I'm going to fix lunch and leave it for the kids. I left and went downtown. (. . .) I don't want to squander what I am earning. I want to spend within certain limits. When I receive money from the publisher I deposit it in the bank. Here are the amounts of money I have deposited in the bank:

```
  248,500.00
  280,000.00
  255,000.00
  150,000.00
  458,000.00
  ───────────
1,391,500.00
```

I bought furniture, clothes, and household utensils. I ate as much as I felt like eating. Beef, fish, grapes, olives, cod, and cheese. When I was in the favela I would think, Oh, if only I could eat cod! Those things used to be just abstract concepts to me but now they are concrete reality. I bathe every day in a shower with hot water and I sleep on my spring mattress.

December 11   Some days I haven't written anything. I was worried and afraid that I would hurt someone with my diary writing. I received a visit from a teacher from Campinas. He told me he teaches sewing. He invented a method of cutting and sewing and he told me that even people who are illiterate can learn it. He wants me to loan him Cr$50,000 so he can open a workshop. I told him I couldn't lend it to him.

"I'll sign promissory notes."

He worried me so much about it that I invited him to go downtown to talk to Dr. Lélio. I cursed my life. When I didn't have any money I was never able to be at ease because hunger kept me wrapped up in its black cloak. Now I have money and I still don't have any peace because of the opportunists, the pirates that try to take advantage of my situation. They see books being sold and think that all the profits are mine. I get a commission on sales.

Dr. Lélio told the tailor from Campinas that there was no way to honor his request. He showed Dr. Lélio his models. I thanked God when Dr. Lélio dismissed us. Back in the street the man kept on pestering me. I am fed up with these nuisances that continue to plague me. (. . .) I began to earn money, and the octopuses began to appear, waving their tentacles. Why don't they ask for money from Ligth [Light, the power utility], from Count Francisco Matarazzo? There are people that don't need money and they come and ask me to give them something. I never asked for anything out of ambition. When I asked for help, I asked for what was essential. Leftovers for my kids to eat, shoes for Vera.

The tailor told me that he had found someone to help set up the factory and that the profits would be divided. I said no. He wants to arrange for money to set up the factory and the profits will go exclusively to him, the inventor.

Selfish. The selfish person thinks he ought to live alone in the world. If his invention makes money he can form a corporation. If Nature is collective, why is it that man has to be selfish? He wants everything just for himself. An orange tree produces oranges for thousands of people. The sun is a unique star and it warms the whole world.

. . . Sometimes I get to thinking, In the favela there is brutality. They were rough and unpolished. Here there are rivalries, ambition. There is no sincerity. The man from Campinas took me to a notary public to draw up a promissory note for Cr$50,000. But Dr. Lélio wouldn't lend him the money.

I had never heard of a promissory note. I was the one that bought the stamps for the document; that's because the tailor from Campinas didn't have any money. I left him and returned to Osasco. (. . .) There are people that hate me, saying, "That despicable woman is rich."

December 12   Divina, the daughter of my maid, Dona Maria, asked me to lend her Cr$100. (. . .) Dona Maria works for me. When I have guests she becomes sad and displeased and grumbles, "My God in heaven, the world's coming to an end! God is punishing me. The world is turned upside down. I, a white woman, have a black woman for a boss." (. . .)

I let out a big laugh and thought, We blacks don't revolt just because we have a white boss. (. . .) I'm not very demanding of my maids. I don't make an issue of color. I like Dona Maria because she washes clothes really well.

December 13 . . . I bought two straw hats for walking along the beaches in Recife. When we arrived at the airport the porters greeted me saying, "You don't stop. You want to see the whole world!"

"I want to visit the cities of Brazil."

We took off at eleven o'clock. The passengers recognized me and greeted me. (. . .) At twelve noon we arrived in Rio.

. . . We had a quick lunch because the plane was going to take off. . . . At 6:00 P.M. we arrived in Bahia. We stopped to eat dinner. I wanted to see Bahia, the country's first capital. But the airport is a long way from the city. A young man that was on the plane said to the waiter, "This is Carolina Maria de Jesus."

Within three minutes a reporter arrived to do a story. (. . .) We got on the plane and it took off. At 9:00 P.M. we arrived in Recife. The reporters were waiting for us. They were wearing light-weight clothes. Several people asked for autographs. I was photographed with the blonde millionaire from the United States, Mary Johnson. I was visiting Recife at the invitation of the noble and illustrious mayor Miguel Arraes. The Guararapes Airport was overcrowded. I was asked what I thought of the trip.

"The flight was very good. I am happy to get to know the people of the Northeast."

. . . The reporter and I got in Sr. Fernando Navarro's car and we went to do a TV program. I was interviewed by Sr. Helio Polito. We were introduced to the people of Recife on TV. I greeted the citizens of the state of Pernambuco and I thanked everyone for their friendly welcome. After the program was over we went to the Grande Hotel. The reporters were waiting for us. I was happy and confused with the friendliness of the northeasterners. What well-bred people!

. . . They asked me what I thought of communism.

"I haven't read about communist countries and I haven't been to any, so I can't give an opinion."

They said I was a communist because I pity the poor and the workers that don't earn enough to live on. They don't have a true defender unless it's the strike, a means they resort to in order to improve their living conditions. But they are so unfortunate that they wind up getting arrested and fired from their jobs. Conclusion: the worker doesn't have the right to say that he's going hungry.

When men become supereducated they will free up the land and whoever wants to plant can plant. And there will not be any hunger in the world. The land has to be free just like the sun.

If the sun were on the earth men would unlawfully take possession of it.

December 14 . . . The room where I was staying looked out on a plaza filled with trees. (. . .) I left and went to see the churches and buy newspapers. The streets are well paved. I felt compassion for the northeasterners. Some are poorly dressed, proving that they are poor. I looked at the sad faces of the northeasterners. (. . .)I returned to the hotel. The journalist Alexandrino Rocha informed us that we were going to have lunch with the mayor Miguel Arraes, at the Buraco da Otilia Restaurant.

. . . I received a visit from Sr. Hernani Bezerra, who told me that he was making sacrifices in order to study. I thought it was funny when he said, "When I was a boy my dream was to have bread and butter to eat but I couldn't. And I swore: if some day I'm able, I'm going to eat bread and butter every day."

He looked at me and said, "Carolina, I have gone hungry. That's why I understood your book."

. . . While we were waiting for the time to leave to have lunch with the mayor, I continued to walk around. Listening to the people's comments. (. . .) They all complain about the wealth of São Paulo, the legitimate son of the president of the Republic. São Paulo and Rio are the favorites. The North and the Northeast are adopted children. Undernourished children. (. . .) The Northeast is the garbage dump of Brazil.

. . . At one o'clock we went to have lunch at the Buraco da Otilia. The building is at ground level and made of wood. It is located along the banks of the Capibaribe River. Through the window you can see the river flowing along. (. . .) The food was delicious.

. . . After lunch was over we went along the beach. The ocean is emerald green. Something that I found interesting about northeasterners: they think everything that is green is beautiful. For them green is the symbol of life. I thought the coconut palms were pretty and also the huts covered with coconut palm leaves.

. . . That afternoon we went to autograph books at the Nacional Bookstore and Publishing House. My presence caused people to stop and look at me. Each face I saw was smiling at me. I thought, If only I could live here. . . . The poets Carlos Moreira, Josué de Castro, Paulo Cavalcanti, Audálio Alves, and Ascenço Ferreira were present.

December 15   We got up at six o'clock and were waiting for the station wagon that was going to take us to Caruaru. At nine o'clock Sr. Joacir Fonseca Soares and the driver arrived. We departed. The reporter was happy. (. . .) The youthful Joacir Fonseca was talking and showing his good humor. What intelligent people the North has!

. . . The road is paved all the way. They built gardens with plants resistant to the periods of intense heat. The only flowering tree is the *flamboian* [flame tree], with its red flowers. Northeasterners look at those flowers with expressions of tenderness. They say, "They aren't afraid of the drought."

. . . There are a lot of shacks along the road inhabited by rickety-looking people, requiring food to restore them to health. Those people, punished by Nature, have a stinking existence. (. . .) I thought: even Nature chooses favorites. In the South it rains. In the North it doesn't.

. . . When we arrived in Caruaru we were received cheerfully. I didn't observe any incivility in the northerners. They are so courteous that you can't tell the educated ones from the uneducated. The radio station announced our arrival. Only I didn't have any books to sign. I felt sorry for those people. I thought, They like books and the books are late getting here. They like to plant crops, but it hardly ever rains.

A *zabumba* band was playing in the plaza. I was introduced in a patio where they served cake and beverages. A delicious drink, but I was afraid of getting a little tipsy and not being able to fulfill my obligations. The poet Lycio Neves, who was wearing a suit as white as cotton balls, received us cordially. The members of the *zabumba* band were all poorly dressed, undernourished black people. I thought I was seeing slum dwellers. They smiled, looking at me with great respect. Tender looks. I was seeing these people for the first time and I felt like I had known them for ages. The reporter said to me, "Carolina, here is the gateway to the backlands. The greatest scenes of poverty and deprivation are yet to come."

"Poverty," I kept repeating in my mind. I gave Cr$1,000 to the members of the *zabumba* band. The reporter gave them Cr$1,000. The director of the *zabumba* band said, "We have been to Rio. José Condé is from Caruaru. He came to see us."

. . . We had dinner with the mayor of Caruaru, Sr. Antônio Lyra.

He was seated next to me with his elbows on the table and his head resting in his hands. He didn't have anything to say. He just listened to what others were saying. Criticizing the politicians. There were thirty-five of us at the table. (. . .) It was when we were leaving that I realized that the man who was sitting next to me was the mayor. I was confused, trying to remember what I had said to the mayor.

. . . They gave us some gifts. Little ceramic dolls made by [folk artist] Vitalino. I really liked one of the dolls—the one made to look like a newspaper reporter.

December 16   We said our goodbyes and returned to Recife. (. . .) On the outskirts of town I saw the pipes that were the main water lines. They said that Sr. Juscelino Kubitschek was piping water into Caruaru from forty kilometers away. The people praised the former president of Brazil. And I who had been anti-Kubitschek also became an admirer of the former president of Brazil. And I ask his forgiveness for the stabs I took at him in *Quarto de Despejo*. . . .

. . . At eleven o'clock we arrived in Recife. (. . .) A young man asked me to visit the cancer hospital and the building they have yet to finish. I accepted the invitation. We went to the hospital where I was filmed with the patients. It was the first time I had seen cancer patients, those unlucky people who know they are going to leave this life behind forever. I said, "All of you are going to be cured. They have discovered a medicine that will cure you."

I saw a young man smile. He looked at me tenderly. In the hallway there were more than one hundred people waiting to see a doctor. I was introduced to the doctors, who complained about the delays in funding for hospitals and the lack of equipment. The young man who accompanied me is a journalist for the Diários Associados. He gave me twenty-five policies to sell in order to raise Cr$25,000 for the hospital. We went to see the hospital they are building. Construction was halted for lack of funding.

. . . I returned to the hotel sad and horrified. (. . .)
Sr. Hernani Bezerra was waiting for us. He wanted us to go visit his mother. We went to his house. What a wonderful and comfortable house! (. . .) I told him I was going to be on TV—if we could wait. The reporter was playing with the couple's youngest daughter, telling her she looked like Little Lulu.[31] Sr. Hernani Bezerra's wife prepared a meal for us. What a fine woman.

At 7:00 P.M. we went to watch TV. I was shown visiting the sick and I felt like they were watching, since they have TVs in hospital rooms.

December 17 . . . At seven o'clock we left Recife. (. . .) When we boarded the plane I got my rosary out of my purse, so I could pray. My prayers were for the northeasterners. (. . .) When we got off the plane in Rio I heard some voices saying, "Look at Carolina! She's become important; she's imitating Juscelino [Kubitschek]. She's one of the newly rich. She's going to want to build a house up in space and write a book: *From the Favela to the Moon.*"

I was the object of their stares. I went to phone Dona Jurema Finamour. She wasn't at home. I left a message. Walking around in the airport I saw a brown-skinned woman leading a little girl by the arm and crying. Rich people don't concern themselves with a poorly dressed woman's tears. I asked, "Why are you crying?"

She was frightened when she heard me. She said in a tearful voice, "I'm from Sergipe. My son lives in São Paulo. He asked me to come live with him because his wife died giving birth. And my grandchildren are left without a mother. There are five children. He bought my ticket as far as Rio and I don't have enough money to get to São Paulo and I don't know anybody here in Rio."

Tears were sliding down the woman's cheeks. I said to the director of Lloyd Aéreo [Airline], "Give her a ticket. I'll pay for it."

"The fare is Cr$3,700, with the child."

I counted out the money. I had Cr$5,000. The woman stopped crying and began to smile. And she looked at me curiously as if she were seeing something supernatural. Everywhere I went the woman's eyes followed me.

. . . When we got to São Paulo the woman introduced me to her son and told him what had happened. She said to him, "She was my mother there in Rio. I am never going to forget that lady."

I said goodbye to the woman without asking for her address.

December 18 . . . I went to the real estate office to find out if the house was vacant. Not yet. The relatives of the owner still hadn't found a house.

"But he said the house was vacant."

"You need to be a little more patient."

I left the real estate office, I took a taxi, and I went to see what was going on with the house.

December 20 . . . The real estate agency promised I would get the house on the twentieth. And today is the twentieth. (. . .) I have decided that I am going to spend Christmas in my house no matter what.

December 24 I got up at four o'clock. I kept thinking about all the turmoil in my life. Every day I go to the real estate office to find out when Sr. Carivaldo is going to let me have the house. (. . .) I have decided that I am going to live in my house no matter what. I started getting my clothes and the dishes ready. At daybreak I went to the bar to ask the bar owner if he could possibly arrange for a truck to move my things to 562 Rua Benta Pereira. I went to pay the Japanese man for some things I had bought on credit. I paid the owner of the little grocery store. When the truck arrived I asked the Spaniard if he would drive me to my house in the Alto de Santana district. He told me he wouldn't. He couldn't do it because he was going to the shop. I had José Carlos look for a truck. I went to wake up Dona Maria to help me and to see if she had ironed the clothes yet. I asked her if she wanted to go to [Alto de] Santana. She said "no" because she wanted to spend Christmas at her house. (. . .) She works for me, but she won't drink out of my cups or sample the food from my pans. She is very proud.

. . . José Carlos returned with the truck. The driver, after he saw all the furniture, told me I needed two trucks.

"Can you line up another truck?"

"Sure."

They started to load up the truck. The owner of the little grocery store advised me to send the kids away to a boarding school, saying that I shouldn't neglect my children. I don't like people who interfere in other people's lives. I am working in order to try to rear [my children] properly. (. . .) Dona Rosa came to say goodbye, and she told me that she was sorry I was moving to Santana. She said she would go with me and she went to tell her father. Dona Rosa's father was out in front of my house. I hugged him and said, "He . . . is my boyfriend!"

Dona Rosa smiled and said, "Marry him, Dona Carolina. He's a widower."

The drivers were starting up their engines. I bought a little writing desk from Sr. Victor, the furniture store owner and my landlord. I agreed to go pay him later. He was really good to me. He is an upright man. He has a beautiful quality—his word. Sr. Antonio Soeiro Cabral had given me the desk I had been using. When I got ready to move, he came and got it. I told him, "What kind of a man are you? Isn't your word any good? You gave me the desk three months ago and now you're coming to get it."

He was the one who brought me to Osasco. He treated me really well in his house. It was the only place I had ever lived well.

But we didn't see things the same way. There are certain things that happen that can break up a friendship. . . . When I give somebody something, it's theirs.

. . . When we got in the truck the neighbors were looking at us. (. . .) Now that I have gotten rich I ask God to not let me be ambitious. I got in the truck with the heavy furniture. Dona Rosa went in the other truck with the light-weight furniture. The truck carrying the lighter furniture is newer. It went first and was going pretty fast. The older truck came behind as if it had rheumatism. (. . .) We had problems getting there. When we were arriving, I missed the street the house is on. Dona Rosa said that the *Baiana* [woman from the State of Bahia] was cursing.

. . . I paid the drivers Cr$4,000. Dona Rosa went back in the truck. The neighbors were saying that I shouldn't have moved without letting them know. I was nervous because I don't like people giving me advice on what to do. (. . .) I decided to go downtown. I took a taxi. I was nervous. I was dirty and people were greeting me on the street. The *Folha de São Paulo* newspaper had printed that I was rich. The paper asked what I was going to do tonight. I said I was going to move into my house and send Cr$25,000 to the Campaign to Combat Cancer.

. . . I left the bookstore and went to the real estate office to let Sr. João know that I had already moved. He smiled. (. . .) I went to have lunch in the restaurant near the bookstore. I ordered feijoada. While I was eating, some young people asked me to sign autographs for them. I bought two books—*O Pequeno Principe [The Little Prince]* and *O Homem ao Quadrado* [Man squared] by Leon Eliachar. I showed my book to the young people. They looked it over and gave it back to me. When I finished eating I paid Cr$240 and returned home. (. . .) People stopped to greet me and wish me Merry Christmas.

. . . When I arrived I found a man from the North talking to Sr. [Alfredo] Monteiro.[32] When I went inside the man that was talking to Sr. Monteiro looked at me sarcastically. I stared back at him. He wanted to stop me from entering the house.

"I bought this house! Senhor Carivaldo told me that the house was empty. I was supposed to move on the twentieth."

The man changed his attitude. He changed completely. I went to eat. I was sleepy, and I wanted to clean out a room for myself. The man wouldn't allow it. In order to avoid trouble I decided to stay in the living room.

. . . In the afternoon Sr. Monteiro's children arrived and began to ask, "What the devil is all this?"

"It's the woman that bought the house."

An angry black woman arrived and gave me a hateful look, as if I were invading a sacred temple. The neighbors were talking to one another about what was going on. A young neighbor came to see me and set up the metal drum of gas for the stove. (. . .) We ate, I took a bath, and I went to bed. But the fleas seemed like ants in my bed. I couldn't fall asleep because the boys that live in the house started drinking and dancing. I felt like I was in a night club. They were complaining that my furniture was getting in the way of their dancing. I fell asleep to the loud laughter and the music. I woke up hearing the children wishing their parents Merry Christmas.

December 25 I got up at five o'clock. Today I am sad. I feel like the spark has gone out of my life. I made coffee, went outside and looked at the sky to see if it was going to rain because I pity the slum dwellers. Because the favela is flooded. It's horrible to walk in water. I went to cook beans. Sr. Alfredo Monteiro said to me, "You don't need to cook. Mama will cook for us."

I feel content, because I need to write. I went and sat in the sun. A black man walked by. I greeted him. He looked at me with contempt and did not return my greeting. I cursed him roundly. It seems that this black man is not happy with my success.

The sun was delightful. I began to think about my life. Everybody says that I have become rich. That I have become a happy person. Anybody who says that is fooled. Due to the success of my book I am looked at as a bill of exchange. I represent profit. A gold mine, admired by some and criticized by others. What a mixed-up Christmas for me.

João came looking for me and I asked him to go buy me a

newspaper. The *Estado de São Paulo*, so I could see the ranking of my book. I gave him Cr$10. He ran around in circles and didn't find it. He came back mad. I reprimanded him.

"You're not very bright."

He went out mad. João is going to have a hard time understanding about life because he doesn't like to be criticized. (. . .) A woman passed by. I decided to ask her where there is a newsstand. She showed me. I talked to the woman, and she was happy when I told her that I am Carolina Maria de Jesus.

"Are you the one who writes?"

"Yes I am. I'm living here on Benta Pereira Street."

"How nice! I'm happy to know that you are living here on my street."

The woman wished me a Merry Christmas and went on with her shopping.

I kept on writing. Looking at the people walking along my street. I can say "my street" because I am buying a house here in the neighborhood.

December 26 I woke up at 3 A.M. to write. I made breakfast for the young people [in the house] who are leaving for work. (. . .) I went to buy the *Folha* to see if my interview had been printed. The interview was in the *Folha de São Paulo*.

I showed the article to Sr. Monteiro. He smiled, thinking it was humorous. I decided to go downtown. . . . I dressed my children to go downtown. We got off at Tiradentes Avenue; I went there to see my good old friends. The ones who recognized me kept staring at me with admiration. I went to visit José Castilho because he has helped me a lot. I went to visit Rodolfo Scharauffer because Vera told me she misses him. I went to visit Ivani. She told me she was going to get married. (. . .) Ivani's mother offered to sell me her house. I won't buy it because it is too small.

. . . I decided to go downtown. I passed by *Ultima Hora* and I asked Sr. Remo Pangella to send a check to the Recife Cancer Clinic. When I went to Recife I commiserated with the sick people there.

December 27 I got up at 5 A.M. It was painful to see my furniture scattered everywhere. And to think that I had dreamed of a cinder-block house, hoping that then I would find peace and quiet.

. . . There are those who bother me and those who admire me. Those who want help and those who want money to buy a house.

. . . I went to the butcher shop and I bought a leg of pork for Cr$510. The butcher and I chatted. [I told him], "You seem robust because you live surrounded by meat."

I left the butcher shop and entered a bar. I bought sodas for my children. We got on the bus. I still don't know how to take buses. I got off in the wrong place and we had to walk. The children complained because they don't like to walk [so much]. People who recognized me stopped me to have a chat. When I got home there was a message from Sr. Silva Neto that he was going to visit me at 9 A.M. (. . .) I spent the afternoon reading and writing.

December 28 I am not going to go out because I have an appointment with the journalists. I was amazed when I saw an open-air market set up outside my door. The vendors recognized me because they had seen me on TV. They stared at me. (. . .) I bought cookies for the children. I came back home, fixed some coffee, and started writing. Journalist Silva Neto arrived at 9 A.M. along with the photographer. He photographed me at home and at the open-air market. I explained to Silva Neto the conditions under which I bought my house. (. . .) The vendors were happy because their photograph is going to appear in *Manchete* magazine.

. . . A woman named Guiomar visited me. She complained about her husband being unemployed and asked me if I could buy carpentry tools for him. Then he could work, because the woodworking shops only accept workers who bring their tools.

"How much do the tools cost?"

"Cr$40,000."

She went on telling me that her husband is a house painter and just in case I wanted to get my house painted, he could do it. She told me she is a seamstress and asked if I need to have any sewing done. She finished all of the training courses to be a seamstress, and she couldn't understand how her life turned out to be the way it was. (. . .) She is pregnant and invited me to be the godmother of her new baby.

. . . Newspapermen from *Ultima Hora* came here to invite me to go with them through the favela. I was bathing Vera. The electrician was here fixing the showerhead because it gave shocks when it was turned on. He charged me Cr$100. I gave him Cr$500 and he kept it because he had no change. I asked the reporter named Magalhães to pay. [Then] I left with the reporters. The neighbors gaped at me with curiosity. (. . .) I rode in the newspaper's jeep and saw the places where I used to go when I scavenged for papers in the streets. My neighbor from the favela recognized me in the car. When I got there I went to talk with the wife of a municipal garbage man who had won the federal lottery. The favelados gathered around to see me. They looked at me admiringly.

December 29   . . . I went to the reporter's home. (. . .) My old problem with starvation doesn't exist anymore, thank God! And thanks to the reporter, too. But there are other people who weren't lucky enough to be born with my talent for thinking.

. . . I said goodbye to the reporter and I told him, "I like you very much."

I got on a bus feeling renewed. When I got off the bus I walked home. I passed by a store and looked at the bolts of cloth in the window. They are beautiful.

"Are you Dona Carolina?"

"Yes, I am."

"Thank you for choosing my neighborhood to live in."

I said goodbye and went along thinking. I was unhappy about being popular.

"Look at Carolina Maria de Jesus!"

"Oh, her! That woman is worth a fortune."

A black boy called to me, "Dona Carolina!"

I entered the barbershop to see what he wanted. He looked at me full of admiration. (. . .) I said goodbye, wishing him a happy 1961.

I hurried along Alfredo Pujol Street. I turned off onto another street because I glimpsed trees of thick lush foliage. Where there are trees, there are birds. I love birds because they are pleasant. They don't have the perversity men do—men whose evil minds built the atomic bomb and other useless things. Those inventions are made to intimidate nations.

. . . A woman who wrote a book in Yiddish came to get me to take her downtown because she wanted to show her book to Dr. Lélio. She wants him to get it translated and published.

. . . We took a bus. It was full. When I was going to pay the fare, somebody had already paid it for me. I don't know who did it, but I thank this secret friend. I headed for the bookstore. There were some people there, in a state of activity. My book was just arriving—the seventh printing.

I took the elevator. Sr. Paulo Dantas was at the bookstore. I asked him to greet the Jewish writer. He looked at the manuscripts and told her it would be impossible to publish them because they were in another language. He sent her to talk to Dr. Lélio.

December 30 . . . I sent José Carlos to buy the *Ultima Hora* to read the latest happenings in the city. A couple came here to ask me to donate to a shelter being built for favela children. She is going to build it in Itapecirica da Serra.[33] She said goodbye and I got dressed and left the house. I went to the bookstore.

. . . I went with the reporter. We met Helena Silveira, a writer. The reporter introduced me to her and she told me that the writer Jurema Finamour was at the Excelsior Hotel. I was happy. I said goodbye to the reporter and stayed with Dona[34] Helena Silveira. She met friends along the way. At Dom José de Barros Street we met a black man[35] with an enigmatic look.

She told him, "This is Carolina."

He hugged me and kissed me. People who were passing by stopped in their tracks and looked at us petrified. I was troubled by those looks. "Who was that man?" I asked because I wanted to understand why everyone was staring.

"It is Vice-Governor Porfírio da Paz."

"Oh!" I cried, astonished and overwhelmed.

In an instant I started remembering my life's history. From a maid, a peasant, a paper scavenger, to an admired writer who was kissed by the vice-governor! I even started to think about writing a samba song including this scene of me with Sr. Porfírio da Paz.

We said goodbye and went on our way. When we got to the Excelsior Hotel, the desk clerk told us that there was no Jurema Finamour there. But he looked in the files anyway. He located a Jurema and called her. Dona Helena Silveira talked to her. She invited us up to her apartment.

December 31 . . . When day broke I asked João to go buy a copy of *Ultima Hora.* I wanted to see who was elected 1960 "Man of the Year." Sr. José Bonifácio [a politician] won. I received eight votes and Audálio one, the one I cast for him. I felt sorry for him because he received only my vote. . . . I spent the day in bed. I wanted to listen to the radio so I would know who had won the [annual] São Silvestre race. Every year is so different. Last year I was in the favela. This year I am in a cinder-block house. Since I was eight years old I have been looking for tranquillity and happiness.

There are those who believe that the human soul is never satisfied.

Brazil, 1961, and places of residence of Carolina Maria de Jesus (inset). Adapted, with permission, from Robert M. Levine, The Vargas Regime: The Critical Years, 1934–1938 *(New York: Columbia University Press, 1970), 19 and Robert M. Levine and José Carlos Sebe Bom Meihy,* The Life and Death of Carolina Maria de Jesus *(Albuquerque: University of New Mexico Press, 1995), 22.*

Carolina and Audálio Dantas in Canindé favela, São Paulo, 1960. (Photograph courtesy of Audálio Dantas.)

Carolina in her favela shack, 1960. (Photograph courtesy of Vera Eunice de Jesus Lima.)

Carolina and Vera at a fashion show, about 1961. (Photograph courtesy of Vera Eunice de Jesus Lima.)

Carolina playing the guitar, about 1961. (Photograph courtesy of Vera Eunice de Jesus Lima.)

Carolina at a book-signing reception, 1960. (Photograph courtesy of Vera Eunice de Jesus Lima.)

January 1, 1961 . . . I was all alone with my kids. They were comfortable. Vera said, "It would be great if we could live by ourselves."

. . . I've been having a lot of visitors lately. Some come to ask for money, others just want to meet me. When the doorbell would ring the kids would say, "Mama's not here."

I decided to clean house. I was boiling water to kill roaches when the doorbell rang. João went to the door and said I wasn't home. I went to the door and looked through the glass.

"What is it you want?"

"Carolina, I've come to kiss your feet. Can I come in?"

I didn't invite him in because he was drunk. And drunks are big talkers. They talk on and on and don't say anything.

"I can't ask you in because I have to go to the TV station."

"That's alright. I know you just don't want me to come in. You left the favela and now you're rich. . . . Now you're Dona Carolina."

I closed the door feeling sorry for him, because I don't like to hurt anybody's feelings.

. . . I kept on cleaning the house and thinking about my life. I am getting old. I cleaned the bathroom. The house looked nice. At seven o'clock I went outside to wash the front of the house. A man arrived who had come looking for me a few days ago. He asked me to go talk to *Ultima Hora* to get them to sponsor a program on TV. He wanted to have a discussion about the people in the favelas.

"But *Ultima Hora* is not going to listen to me. You are the one that needs to go talk to them."

"I don't have the prestige that you have."

"I can't help you."

"I've come to see you with the best of intentions and you let me down!"

The man left without even saying goodbye. I was scared. What if the man tried to break into my house?

January 2 . . . Today I'm sad. (. . .) I left the house somehow or other. While I was waiting for the bus I talked to a black man who has a mattress shop. I complained, telling him that I was rebelling against the way things were turning out and that I wanted to go to Rio Grande do Sul.

"You've become famous. Everywhere you go now you're going to see things you don't like."

. . . I stopped at the newsstands to find out what was going on in the world. "Cuba is at war" was the big news. I have no praise for the man that makes war because war destroys what he builds.

. . . We went back home on the bus. (. . .) Tomorrow the TV station is sending a crew here to the house.

January 3 . . . At 2 P.M. the car from TV Record arrived. They started to get ready for the broadcast. The kids and neighbors crowded around the entrance gate. I took a bath and got the kids ready. I went to buy *pinga* and coffee. I'm going to fix drinks of *pinga* and lime for the reporters. I have two bottles of wine. I borrowed wine glasses from the neighbors. (. . .) I went to talk to the neighbor to pass the time. She and her husband, Sr. Rogerio Reis, they are good neighbors. João came to tell me that the reporter had arrived. I went to greet him. (. . .) The reporter Murilo Antunes Alves arrived. When the program started the house and front yard were supercrowded. Sr. Murilo Antunes Alves asked me why I have a picture of [President] Jânio Quadros.

"I'm not a supporter of Janio. I keep Sr. Jânio Quadros's picture to see if he will continue to smile till the end of his term."

Sr. Murilo Antunes Alves praised my book and mentioned that it deals with a social problem. When the TV crew left, I went to talk to Sr. Rogerio. (. . .) I went to bed at 2 A.M.

January 4 . . . Since I bought the house I have reached the conclusion that I am important. I am happy. Now I'm somebody and I can receive visitors. I spent the day lying down. At six o'clock I remembered Dona Suzana Rodrigues's invitation to be on her TV program. I got ready and left in a hurry. When I arrived at the studio the show was already on the air. I managed to get on.

. . . When we left the TV station Dona Suzana Rodrigues invited us to go to the Clube dos Artistas. I saw several tables where there were men but no women. We sat at the biggest table. Dona Suzana ordered dinner: *picadinho* [minced meat]. They served eggs, rice and manioc. (. . .) Several people saw me and remarked, "That's Carolina."

Dona Suzana Rodrigues graciously introduced me to her friends. Her son and daughter were with us. Dona Suzana invited a man to come to our table. She introduced us, "This is the writer Mario Donato."

. . . He said to me, "Carolina, use your money wisely, because you can't make a living off of literature."

. . . I managed to get rich off of my book. My book was the fairy that transformed me from a Cinderella into a princess. My dreams are becoming reality. I wanted a cinder-block house. And I got it. What is really moving is to insert the key in the lock and open the door, knowing that the house is mine. There are times I feel like shouting loud enough to be heard all throughout the Universe,

Long live my book!

Hurrah for my two years of schooling!

And hurrah for books, because they're the things I love the most, other than God.

January 5 . . . The house has two floors. The rooms are big: two bedrooms. The view is magnificent. I can see the Cantareira Mountains in the distance.

. . . I took the bus and was thinking about Sr. J. F. Bueno, who lives on Guaporé Street. He is unemployed, he owes two months rent, and he owes money to the store. The one that came to see me the first time was his wife. She came to ask for money because she's pregnant. She complained that her husband is a cabinet maker and he doesn't have tools to work with. She wanted to know if I could pay the money owed the store. I sent her a note that I was going to pay the store on Friday. But I wasn't able to do it. She showed up with her husband and made a list of the tools I should buy him so he could work:

> 1 plane
> 1 medium-sized hand saw
> 1 small saw
> 1 small square
> 1 medium-sized hammer
> 1 file
> 6 chisels
> 1 compass
> 1 drill
> 4 drill bits
> 1 triangle file

I'm going crazy with all these requests.

January 6 . . . I received a visit from a woman who wants to build a children's home—Christian Union for Aid to Children. They have a tract of land in Itapecirica da Serra, and they want to build an educational institution for maladjusted children. (. . .) She invited me to invest. We agreed that she should come back on Tuesday. I'm upset and agitated, thinking about the ups and downs in my life. Every day I find myself disgusted about something.

January 7 . . . Sr. Fabio Paulino and his wife came to see me. They got married a week ago. She is a teacher. She's distinctive and very pleasant. He is a broadcaster for the Cometa and Ninth of July [radio] stations. They are my neighbors.

January 8 . . . A man who said he was from Paraná came to ask me to loan him Cr$800,000 because he took out a loan at the bank and the notes are due and he doesn't have the money to pay them.

(. . .) He told me that he could wait until Tuesday for me to give him the money. I was horrified. Where am I going to get Cr$800,000 to loan to a total stranger three days from now?

He told me he would deposit Cr$100,000 in the bank for me every month. If he is able to deposit that amount in the bank to pay his debts, why doesn't he just pay back the bank?

He left. I promised to go see him in the Piratininga Hotel, where he's staying. He told me that his request shouldn't be divulged, because he's an important person. In my humble opinion he's a beggar fantasizing that he's a rich person.

. . . Several people came to see me. I'm sad because the house is a mess. A man who lives in the Vila Mariana district came to buy a book from me. A little black man was at the door when a couple was leaving. He came in. He showed me pictures of his relatives, his wedding, and so on. I was thinking to myself, He is the type that wants to have class.

January 9   I got up mad, cursing my life. I am unhappy with this house. I look at the walls, and they're dirty. I look at the front yard, and it's sad-looking because there are no flowers. The room that has the northerners' furniture in it is overrun with fleas. I tried to go in there and the fleas attacked my legs. This is just too much. I'm going to solve my problems. I'm not going to continue like this. I wrote a note to Sr. Antonio: "The reporter Audálio Dantas stated that if you don't claim your furniture by tomorrow he is going to haul it to the Municipal Warehouse. Then you can settle up with the mayor."

. . . I cursed the reporter. That dog could have gotten me a clean house. (. . .) I didn't want this house, but the reporter had his way. He overrules everything that I want to do. But I have to put up with it. He was the one who helped me out, so for that reason he prevails. But on May 13 [holiday celebrating the abolition of slavery] he is going to give me my freedom.

. . . I looked around the living room. Thinking about some carpeting and a pretty dining room. I counted the nineteen steps that lead to the bedrooms. I picked up my bag and went out. I saw

José Carlos in the street. He ran thinking that I was coming to get him. I went to talk to Dona Elza. My thoughts were all jumbled up.

January 10 . . . I bought some steel wool. I'm going to clean up the room that's going to be for the kids. I cleaned up the back yard. I made coffee. I didn't have time to cook lunch. I cleaned the window panes and the blinds. The house is well built. It's just that they've practically destroyed it. I worked all day and all night to clean up this house. The floor looked nice.

January 11 . . . I went to the open-air market. The women asked me if the northerners had moved out yet.

"No. They promised to move today."

I bought a shirt for João to wear to school. Dezuita came with a woman to pick up the furniture. (. . .) Sr. Monteiro hauled off his furniture. The truck didn't stop at the door because of the market. I gave a sigh of relief when I saw that the house was all mine. I didn't know that I would suffer so many annoyances in buying the much-longed-for cinder-block house. (. . .) I thought, When I buy a house I'm going to talk about the flowers that will grace my front yard.

. . . I was exhausted. I was getting ready for bed when the doorbell rang. João opened the door, "It's Audálio."

He greeted me. I told him that I was fighting the fleas. I had already waxed the floors in the two bedrooms. He ran up the stairs. He complimented me on the shiny floors. I composed some songs. I sang them for him. He told me they were good.

January 14 . . . I went to see my old friends again. I talked to the tailor. When I used to collect paper he would help me. (. . .) In the district where I used to pick up paper, Ponte Pequena, they hadn't read my book. What they know comes from the newspapers. The people came up close and looked at me with admiration.

"I saw you on TV."

"I saw your picture in the newspapers."

"Has your life gotten better?"

"No, it hasn't gotten any better. I never have any peace so I can write."

Dona Anita invited me to come and chat with her. But I didn't go. Because when I used to pick up paper she would always run away and if she was at the window she would move away from it. One day I told her she didn't need to leave the window when she saw me, that I wouldn't look at her any more. She hurt me deeply. Now it was my turn to hurt her. She is reaping what she sowed.

I said goodbye and kept on looking at the garbage cans in the streets. Remembering when I used to carry around my forty kilo load, bending over one garbage can after another, pulling out paper and tin cans and metal and putting it all in my sack, and Vera would complain that her dream was to dress just like the little girls in the store windows. I think I'm living a dream. Where there are wonderful moments and tragic moments.

. . . Today is Saturday. If I were still picking up paper I would be running all over the place to get more money. If I were in the favela right now, my son João would be in jail. Reflecting on these things I should thank God and the reporter, who has helped me a lot. I don't have to deal with the quarreling and the police cars anymore.

January 15   . . . I had a visit from some blacks from the interior and some others from São Paulo. Some little black women came to see me. One of them is a painter; she advised me to smooth out my hair.

"The reporters won't let me do it."

"Heavens! Do you obey them?"

"He who is not obedient doesn't triumph."

Sr. Rubens, the singer, came to see me. He complained that his wife doesn't treat him right.

"I'm on your side, because I love my children."

He said he is the one who sews on their buttons when they fall off. He lifted his head, staring at the ceiling, and said with a sorrowful voice, "If I could just disappear . . . die a thousand times rather than live like this."

He left. When he was leaving the bed broke, because there were three men sitting on it.

January 16   . . . I went to the bookstore to see Sr. Paulo Dantas. (. . .) We went down Libero Badaró Street. I saw several people carrying placards. The writing on the placards called for raises. (. . .) I stopped to look. I was recognized. They came up to talk to me, "We want raises."

I felt compassion for them, because I had gone hungry before. I was frightened when I heard their voices and saw the crowd carrying placards. It was the firemen and the police [striking for a pay raise]. A man grabbed my arm. I was next to Deputy Ivete Vargas. We talked about all the confusion in São Paulo. The people were shouting, "The [government's] Plan of Action has taken away our bread!"

. . . I didn't intend to join the demonstration. (. . .) We passed near the bookstore. The people were looking at my picture displayed in the front of the bookstore. (. . .) We went to São Francisco Square. The wives of the soldiers were with their children. They must suffer more than the people in the favelas. I don't know what the men are going to do. If they go to work in the fields, the land owner will exploit them; if they join the police force, the government pays them starvation wages.

January 18 . . . A woman came looking for me. She came to ask me for Cr$400,000 to pay the mortgage on her house. She has two months left before she pays it off.

"You lend me Cr$400,000 and I'll pay back Cr$8,000 a month."

"Come back tomorrow. We'll go talk to Dr. Lélio or the reporter."

January 21 . . . The kids feel strange about the change from the favela to the cinder-block house. José Carlos stares at me for long periods of time. To him I'm a heroine because I bought a cinder-block house.

January 25 . . . The reporter arrived accompanied by the photographer George Torok. They came in. (. . .) We went to the favela. I showed them the places I used to go. The streets I used to roam picking up paper. When I arrived at the favela the children started booing. Within five minutes word had spread that I was in

the favela. The people congregated to see me. I spoke with Dona
Esmeralda. She told me that her husband hadn't come back. He
pretended to be crazy and abandoned his family. (. . .) Torok and
I walked around in the favela. What a filthy place. It's inhuman to
let people live like that. I went to see my shack. Seu [Pal] Chico
had made some changes. He had only kept the board where João
had written—"Audálio is ours." The reporter photographed me
with my people, the people of the favela. I went to talk to Sr. Luiz.
He made a request, "You need to be the voice of the favela. Speak
for us."

I realized that the people who live in the favela looked at me
with admiration.

January 26   I got up at four o'clock and went to write. I'm beginning
to like the house. The fleas are disappearing. It's great to write
now that I have electricity. I've got fourteen bulbs in my house.

I went to the bookstore. Dr. Lélio told me he's going to pay me
for two printings tomorrow. He was going to pay me today, but the
reporter went on a trip. I don't want to accept the money if he's not
here. (. . .) I'm going to dine in the home of Deputy Ivete Vargas.
What a sacrifice it is to take a taxi. It was raining. We finally got
one. I gave the address to the driver. He told me that
he had voted for Dona Ivete Vargas three times. And he hasn't
regretted it, because she didn't deceive the voters. She's a great
woman.

"A great woman nowadays is one who takes care of her
children. She has to deal with the astronomical cost of living."

He didn't appreciate my words.

"A great woman is what Dona Ivete is. It's just that you don't
know her. She has helped the people."

I didn't comment because I don't know her. I was from the
garbage dump. Now I'm from the parlor. I'm in the cinder-block
house. In the garbage dump I knew the underdogs, the exploiters,
and the beggars. In the cinder-block house I'm mixed in with
various classes. The rich and those of the middle class.

. . . I invited the driver to pay a visit to Dona Ivete Vargas,
since he is her devoted constituent.

"Ah! She doesn't know me."

"Come with me. She's going to see you."

He told me that he was going to drive around because on rainy days the drivers make more money. When I entered the building several people recognized me and told me which floor to go to. When I reached Dona Ivete's apartment the place was supercrowded. Several men were there. All from the Labor Party. (. . .) She is well bred and very distinguished. She invited me to dinner.

. . . In every corner there was a bronze bust of [former president] Getúlio [Vargas]. She said, "I was crazy about my uncle."

She used some political expressions that I don't know. Listening to them talk about politics I had the impression that I was in another world. (. . .) A couple that was in broadcasting was present. I told them that I was a composer. I sang something for them.

January 27 I got up at six o'clock. The house was dirty. I made coffee; João went to buy bread. I washed some clothes. João told me that the woman that wants to borrow Cr$400,000 was coming and that he was going to tell her that I wasn't at home.

"Tell her I'm here and have her come in."

I acted that way because I didn't want to teach the kids to lie. She came in carrying some packages. She wants to charm me so that I'll pay up her mortgage. But I haven't straightened out my life yet. I feel like I'm carrion and the crows are circling my body. Human crows that want money.

. . . The man who wants to set up a sewing shop returned to ask me to lend him Cr$50,000. I cursed him, telling him that my only obligation is to take care of my children.

January 28 I got up mad. I went to clean up the front yard. The kids were trampling the ground and the paving stones. I cursed at Vera and José Carlos because they don't appreciate our cinder-block house.

We are free of flooding and vagrants. Our lives have turned

out rosy. Maria Aparecida, the daughter of Dona Elza, wanted to play with Vera, but she's being punished. I took the bus and got off on Tiradentes Avenue. (. . .) I met Dona G. who lives in the back of the store. She invited me to come in. She told me she was pregnant.

That's a lie. She's still slim as a worm.

I kept on gazing at those places where I used to go looking for cans, scrap iron, and paper to sell. (. . .) I bought corn meal for the kids to eat with milk. I took a taxi. The driver told me his name is Serafim; he's the son of a washwoman, and he's writing a book in his free time.

"Write the book and give it to the reporter. He's honest."

He continued to talk about his mother. I showed him the house. He told me he's been following my successes on the radio and in the newspapers.

January 30 I got up when I heard the voice of Lelé, the gardener. He had come to do a job for me. I went downstairs. The kids had already gone out to see him. He examined the front yard. He told me he would have some flowers from the Horto Florestal district brought in and planted for me. I showed him the house. He was impressed with the way my life had improved. And he told me, "So your star has finally shone. You really have left behind the garbage cans."

He promised to come on Wednesday. (. . .) The kids are misbehaving a lot. I spanked them for jumping out my bedroom window to get outside. They broke a bathroom ornament.

January 31 I got up at 9 A.M. when I heard Lelé, who had come to work in the yard. He brought me a coconut palm. He's going to plant it in the middle of the front yard. (. . .) Lelé said, "I wanted to marry you. But you didn't want to. I'd be well off today."

"But if I had married you, I wouldn't have achieved anything."

I paid Lelé, who, looking at me admiringly said, "You really made a leap forward in life! You came out of hell and now you're in heaven."

"You're mistaken. I'm in purgatory."
He promised to come back to see how the flowers were doing.

February 1 Today is João's birthday. He's twelve. He's tall and
starting to fill out. He's in the fourth grade.
. . . Dona A. came. I'm going to see if the reporter has
managed to help her. She is sad. (. . .) I found the reporter at
the newspaper offices. I signed the contracts that are being mailed
to the United States. I asked him if there was any way to get the
money for Dona A. He told me there wasn't, because I have to pay
the installments on the house and what I'm making isn't enough. I
need to buy furniture and put my kids in a boarding school.
. . . Dona A. was sad. She started complaining. She said, "If I
don't get this money, I'm going to kill myself."
"Your husband's got to help you. The dumbest thing you can
do is mortgage your house."

February 4 . . . Someone knocked at the door. It was a black
woman. I told her to come in. She told me she's read all the stories
about me. Her name is Isolina. The woman's a big talker. She told
me she has been sick twenty-two years. She said, "I've only paid two
years on the land I bought. I'm eight years behind in my payments.
The company wants to take the land. They let me stay there because
I was sick. They are demanding that I pay Cr$44,000 all at once.
I've come to ask you to pay off the land for me. Then I will pay you
back a little at a time. If I can't pay you back, the land will belong
to you or your kids. The water there is good. My well found water
at a depth of two meters. All the houses are made of cinder-block.
Mine is a shack. Nobody wanted to give me water. The other wells
are sixteen meters deep and mine only goes down two meters. One
neighbor dug a well in the direction of mine and he didn't find
any water. God is on the side of the poor. The lawyer told me to
keep the money until the end of the month."
I gave her a bowl of chicken soup. And an orange. Dona Maria
José was making biscuits and gave her some. I told her I would go
see if I could pay off the land for her. She's going to come back on
the fifteenth.

As soon as she left it began to rain. . . . I gave her Cr$50 to pay for her transportation. (. . .) It was 7 P.M. when a car stopped at the door. The founders of the Christian Union for Aid to Children Orphanage got out. Two women, two men, and two little girls. Vera opened the door for them. They invited me to go on TV to ask for assistance for the construction of a shelter in Itapecirica da Serra. They showed me stories about it in several newspapers from the capital and the interior. (. . .) They are going to establish an orphanage and open a register of donations. A man in the newspaper said that Carolina Maria de Jesus is donating Cr$100,000. I was horrified, because I didn't authorize anyone to say that. I didn't say anything about it. (. . .) São Paulo takes in a host of rascals from the streets. But they can come ask me for money till they're blue in the face.

February 5 . . . We took a taxi. Two little girls rode with me to Radio Nacional. (. . .) I thought it was funny when I asked the doorman at the radio station, "Is Sr. Mario Brasini here?"

He looked me over cautiously and said, "Yes, Doutor Mario Brasini is here. Go to the next street over."

And that's how I found out that Sr. Mario Brasini is a doctor. I went one street over. The doorkeeper, a young woman, told me that Doutor Mario Brasini was on the third floor. We went in. I found him writing. He's skinny. He said to me, "Oh, Carolina!"

"When should I come by to sign the books?"

"After Carnival."

. . . I said goodbye. (. . .) We went to a bar. A young man recognized me and told me he's known me since 1952, when Pacheco wrote a story [about my poetry] in *Ultima Hora*. We began to talk about my popularity. A young man approached saying he had recorded the samba "Favela do Canindé" and asked if I had heard the record.

. . . We took a taxi. When we got to my house I paid the fare and went to look for my kids. I went to see if Vera was in Sr. Rogerio Reis's house. He is very well mannered. He takes in my kids without being haughty. I have good neighbors. Dona Maria José and her husband Sr. José Simões Paulino live at Number 566.

Dona Ivette Oddone lives at Number 600 and Dona Jaci Villar
Miranda at Number 608. And Sr. Aniz Kassabian lives at Number
597. And Dona Elza Bertolini Lopes at Number 575.

The kids were at the home of some good black people, who live
on Francisca Biriba Street. They have a television.

February 6   I opened the window. The sun, the king star, was already
visible. (. . .) I got Vera ready and we went out. I went to the
bookstore. The bookstore's lawyer was present. They added up how
much I had made counting all seven printings of my book. The
reporter told me I spend too much.

Before, I didn't have anything. [So now] I had to buy
everything. If I'm spending money, I'm spending what's mine.
(. . .) His unfair observations upset me. I received two checks.
Audálio told me to put them in the bank. I went to the bank,
deposited the money and withdrew Cr$10,000 to buy some little
boots for Vera. Audálio told me I buy shoes every day. . . .
If he keeps on annoying me, I'm going to go back to picking
up paper.

. . . I went in the store and bought some boots for Vera.
Cr$780. That's a lot to spend on a child's feet.

. . . I was trying to get a taxi when I heard my neighbor
Sr. Fabio Paulino's voice. The cars that were passing were all
occupied. Finally we got a taxi. The driver was black. I told him I
was happy with the actions of the president of the United States,
Sr. Kennedy, because he was abolishing prejudice. Sr. Fabio
Paulino doesn't think very highly of North Americans. He thinks
they are inhumane to the black race.

"Are you Carolina?" the driver asked, looking at me in the
rear view mirror.

"Yes, I am."

He offered his congratulations.

When we arrived Dona Rosa was waiting for me. (. . .) I
complained to Dona Rosa that I was disgusted with life. The favela
was a better place for writing. I didn't have an endless parade of
visitors coming by. I was ignored.

February 7 . . . Last night a young man came from the Christian Union for Aid to Children Orphanage. He wanted me to go with him to the newspapers to speak to Sr. Mauricio Loureiro Gama to make a fund-raising appeal on television. But I refused to go with him because I was exhausted. I'm mad at them for going around announcing that I was going to give them Cr$100,000. Is it possible that I will have to solve all the problems that afflict the Brazilian people? My desire is to aid those that suffer, but I'm powerless to help them.

February 8 I woke up at two o'clock and began to write. That's the time I enjoy because I know that nobody is going to come asking for a loan. With all those people asking for money I'm becoming neurotic. I was startled by the voices and noises I heard. It was the open-air market that comes to my street on Wednesdays. I opened the window and greeted the vendors.

"Are you up yet?"

"I'm writing. I need to have my book ready by September."

. . . The day dawned with the bright lights of the king star. I bathed and made coffee. I grabbed my bag and went to look around in the market. I bought some pens for José Carlos and Vera. José Carlos found Cr$210. I said to Levi, my neighbor, "When I used to live in the favela we never found a dime."

I bought some plates, some glasses, and two cups. Prices are rising and the governments are sleeping.

. . . My neighbor told me that there was a woman at my door. I went to attend to her, inviting her to come in. She told me she has an unfinished house and wanted me to lend her Cr$300,000 so she could finish building it. She said that afterward she was going to rent it and make payments to me at the bank. Her husband is a police lieutenant. I told her I couldn't help her.

"I'm going to board my kids and I need money to pay for their schooling."

But the woman said, "Help me, Dona Carolina. Have pity on me."

She told me some of the awful things the police officers

have to put up with at the hands of the government. What an embarrassment for government officials to be asking for handouts!

. . . The woman gave me her address and asked me to visit her and see her house. She already has a house. And she's not happy. And the poor slum dwellers are happy with a wooden shack. They aren't thinking about putting up a building for the income it would give them. They don't worry people to death asking them for money. Nobody talks about the bank. They don't even know what a check is.

Is it possible that this woman can't be content with what she has? (. . .) The woman went away telling me that if necessary she would go ask the reporter to get me to lend her the money.

February 9 Today nobody came to ask for money. Thank God!

February 10 I got up ready to go. I washed clothes, cleaned up the house, and opened the windows. The air rushed in penetrating the house. I looked at the hilltops all around: Jaraguá Peak, the Cantareira Mountains.

Dona Zezé wanted to feed me lunch. I wouldn't let her because I have food left over from yesterday. I got the kids ready. (. . .) We went to the editorial office. I was looking at the newsstands. The big news: I was horrified by the oppression in Africa. Africa is the land of black people, but the whites went there to take the land away from those poor folks. I think white people interfere in the lives of blacks to cause confusion. It leaves those poor people totally destroyed. I was sorry about Patrice Lumumba [assassinated leader in the Congo], who was able to live a few more days. When will civilization prevail?

. . . When I arrived at the newspaper offices I saw all the journalists gathered together. I greeted all of them and went to speak to Audálio.

"I came to pay the installment on the house."

I gave him the checkbook, and he added up what I had spent, reprimanding me because I spend too much. I told him I want to board my kids and I want to go to work.

"What kind of work do you want?"

"On the radio."

"Oh no!"

He filled out the check.

. . . We waited for the bus. When I arrived I went to return the gold watch that I had bought from Dona Elza, because I can't give her the Cr$25,000. I swore I wouldn't buy anything else because of the way the reporter has criticized me. He's a detective prying into my life. But I'm just going to publish *Casa de Alvenaria* [The cinder-block house]. After that, I'm going to stop.

. . . When I see somebody at my door, I think, That person has come to ask for money. I don't get visits from the folks at the overnight shelter, the soup kitchen at the synagogue on Casemiro de Abreu Street, or the bread line at the Church of the Immaculate Conception. They must be envious of me. And I'm envious of them.

. . . I bought some sausage and returned home. As I was arriving I saw Lelé at the door. He was talking about the yard, that the soil was weak and the plants wouldn't grow. He said, "I need to talk to you in private. You look pretty with that handkerchief tied around your head. I've wanted to marry you for the last eight years, but you wouldn't have me."

I told him, "If I were to get married, it would have to be to a good man who was refined and educated."

"But I am intelligent, don't you think?"

And he asked me to lend him Cr$1000 because his mother is sick and she could get worse at any minute.

"I'll pay you back by working for you."

I told Lelé that I was going to have dinner at Maria do Carmo's house. I closed the door and went away tired, wanting to lie down. (. . .) It's terrible not to have peace of mind. There are times I want to beat up the people that come and bother me.

February 12 Today is Sunday. Carnival. It's a sad-looking day. [But] I am happy. I went shopping, washed clothes, and made coffee. I'm not going to go out.

. . . I bought milk for the kids. I can see changes in them.

They are learning some manners. Seeing them well behaved has given me a resurgence of hope. I hope they are good in the future.

February 14 . . . Dona Ivete complained about my kids writing bad words on her wall. If bad words didn't exist, no one would take note. The main thing is for people to know how to read. (. . .) I'm upset because my kids get accused whenever anything bad happens on our street.

February 15 . . . I took a bath and went to town to see if I could find the reporter. (. . .) I headed for the newspaper offices. I stopped at the newsstands to read about the assassination of Patrice Lumumba. I'm thinking, God has given all people a native land. Africa for blacks, but he made one mistake—filling men with ambition. What a wicked thing to kill the black man in his own country! But the natives will wind up prevailing. A few of them will eventually convince the rest.

The journalists asked me why they never see me anymore on the street.

"I've been cleaning up my shack."

"Are you still living in a shack?"

"Oh, I'm still in the habit of saying that. I lived twelve years in a shack."

February 17 I got up at 5 A.M. The kids are going to school. I prepared breakfast and went shopping. João and José Carlos go in the morning. Vera goes in the afternoon. The house is a mess. The kids walk in the mud and get the steps dirty. I fixed lunch: rice, beans, and meat. The thing that I used to fear has ended: "Mama, what are we going to eat today?"

I washed clothes and got Vera ready to go to school. I was going in circles when Dona A. arrived. She told me that she had hurt her foot on a nail. She's sad because she didn't get the money to pay off the mortgage. She told me she wants to work for me. She ironed the clothes and helped me clean the house.

. . . I wrote a note to the reporter, informing him that we were going on Radio Cometa. And asking him to invite the writer Paulo Dantas.

. . . I took a taxi because the electric buses were not running due to the energy shortage. (. . .) When Paulo Dantas arrived we decided that the poet Solano Trindade should accompany us. He told us that he was going out to participate in a demonstration in memory of Patrice Lumumba, the black man who became more powerful after death. We took a taxi to Radio Cometa. The program was terrific. We talked about Brazilian folklore. The one who talked about music was Solano Trindade. Paulo Dantas talked about my talent, about how I write without stopping. When the program was over we thanked the radio personnel and Sr. Fabio Paulino.

February 18 I got up at five o'clock to get the kids ready to go to class. I made coffee. João and José Carlos got themselves ready to go. I went to buy bread. The market stalls were already set up. I bought a set of aluminum canisters to store food in. I paid Cr$720 for six canisters. I'm gradually getting my house organized.

. . . Dona . . . [wife of a police lieutenant mentioned in February 8 entry] arrived. She came to ask me if I could get together enough money so that she could renovate her house. She wants to fix up her house in order to rent it. She already has a house to live in.

Dr. Herculano Neves and his wife arrived. He came to give me a copy of his book *I'll Answer You, Carolina* [a book written criticizing *Quarto de Despejo*]. Dr. Herculano gave me a copy to give to the reporter. I gave him the reporter's address. He told me that a lot of people are going to criticize him for writing the book *I'll Answer You, Carolina*. I mentioned to him that several people are trying to get the book.

"I'm selling it in the interior."

As he was leaving he gave me a copy.

I went to see about the police lieutenant's wife who wants money to renovate her house. They boast of having a TV. Instead of buying a television set why don't they build the house they want to put up for rent?

I told her I don't earn a lot of money. She replied, "I'm going to talk to the reporter."

"Talk about what, if I don't have the money?"

She gave me a hateful look, as if I were obligated to loan her money. When she left, I went to see about Dona Olga. She asked if I knew of a clinic that would accept her. I told her she could sleep here in my house and work for me if she wanted to. She accepted the offer and went to fix dinner and wash the dishes.

Lelé arrived. He was complaining that he had been obliged to send his mother to the hospital. He annoys me with his chit-chat. José Carlos asked him, "Why is it that you never came to our house in the favela? It's only now that my mother is rich that you all notice that she exists."

Lelé told him, "I'm a slum dweller, too."

I let out a loud laugh. He started to joke and play with the kids. I asked them to be quiet, because I've got a headache. What an ugly man. He looks like a wooden doll, like Pinocchio. He wanted to take my kids to sleep in his house. José Carlos asked, "Why didn't you invite us to sleep in your house when we lived in the favela during the floods?"

I asked Lelé to leave because I had a headache. He wants to paint my house. I didn't accept his offer because he talks too much. He asked for money for transportation. (. . .) I gave Lelé Cr$25, and he left. I made some tea for my headache. I took a bath and went to bed.

February 19   I got up at six o'clock. Dona Olga was already up and on her feet. She made coffee. I went to buy bread and meat so Dona Olga can make pies. I got the kids ready to go to the movies. Dona Olga is going to work for me. She's going to let her relatives know.

I'm tired. I lay down on the sofa to write. When I get hungry I'll get up and go eat some pie.

February 20   . . . A man who had come from the North arrived. He told me he had read all the stories that mentioned my name. A woman and some young people arrived. They came to meet me and invite me to go to the Protestant church. I promised I would go. The man from Pernambuco said he was an inventor. And that he had invented a medicine that cures all illnesses. But he doesn't know how to explain his invention. My visitors left, and I got ready to go to the newspaper office to talk to the reporter. (. . .) It started to rain. What a rain! When we got to the newspaper office I found the reporter. I introduced the man from Pernambuco. He displayed a paper that tells about his invention. It seems like he wants to be somebody important. People like this are annoying. (. . .) I said goodbye to the journalists.

. . . I tried to get a taxi but was unsuccessful. I went to take the bus but couldn't get on because it was too crowded. The taxis wouldn't stop and the drivers were looking important as if they were demigods. I saw that there was an incredible number of people waiting, so I gave up. I kept on walking around. I heard an advertisement for Sr. Prestes Maia. I thought, These politicians don't waste any time. A station wagon belonging to supporters of Sr. Emilio Carlos was giving rides to those who were going to the Parada Inglesa.

I was standing alongside a well-dressed man. He was wearing a white suit. He was talking to himself. When a car advertising Sr. Cantidio Sampaio went by, he said, "Die, you miserable wretch. You aren't going to improve the lives of the poor people of São Paulo. You have a car, you good-for-nothing politician. You've come to see the people suffering!"

The car campaigning for Sr. Prestes Maia went by. He cursed it, too, "You're despicable, too. All you talk about is urbanization, urbanization. And you bulldoze houses. What the people need is adequate transportation."

I heard each outburst of nonsense! All the while understanding the anguish of those that need transportation. What happened was it rained and the people flocked together after the rain. When the people are nervous, they have to curse somebody. And they curse the politicians. (. . .) The man kept on looking for a way to get a ride.

. . . A car went by. A German caught it to take him to Tucuruvi. I asked him to take me to Voluntarios da Patria Street. He told me, "There's plenty of room."

A Syrian got in and called out, "Tucuruvi, two places."

The car stopped. On Tiradentes Avenue we took on two passengers. I wound up sitting next to an army officer. What a disgusting and unlikable fellow. He took advantage of me and stroked my back. What torture. Traffic was congested. In the car next to us a couple was kissing. A bleached blonde was smoking. The men in my car said to me, "Write this up in your diary, Carolina."

The young girl in the car straightened up. The officer was annoying me. The German didn't want to talk, saying only that he's not much of a conversationalist. He got out to find out the cause of the traffic jam. Time was passing. The Syrian became indignant and started cursing the government. The driver said, "The politicians couldn't have predicted that the population of São Paulo would double like this."

The Syrian was silent. I gave thanks to God when the car started up again.

I got out on Voluntarios da Patria Street. I bought pies and pastries. I went out to the street looking for a ride. A taxi went by, I signaled for him, and he stopped. I asked him to take me home.

"Ah, is it in Imirim? I don't go there."

"Take me, and I'll pay you double."

I got in the car. The driver was complaining about being hungry.

"Go somewhere and eat."

"I don't like to do that."

"You drivers have to eat anywhere you can. You can't go without eating. Your blood pressure drops and you get short of breath."

"It sounds like you have gone hungry before, because you know all those symptoms."

"I used to live in the favela. And the people that live there struggle just to eat."

"Ah, are you Carolina?"

"That's right."

"I'm pleased to meet you."

"Thank you. When you need to call on me, I'm at your service. How many children do you have?"

"Three. Nowadays, it's a struggle to support three kids."

When I got back home I cheered up. The meter read Cr$65. I gave the driver Cr$150. He said to me, "You keep your word. You told me you would pay me double and you did."

The kids were listening to the radio, happy and carefree. João wanted to know, "Why are you so late?"

"The traffic was bad."

"Sr. Fabio walked back. Poor Sr. Fabio Paulino. He walked all the way back here from the City Market."

Dona Olga came in saying that she hitched a ride in a police car.

February 21   I got up at six o'clock. I got the kids ready to go to school. I went to buy bread. When I returned I saw Dona Cilu, a woman who does cleaning for me. I greeted her and asked her in. She came in and went to change clothes. I went out to buy school uniforms. And notebooks for the kids. I bought a uniform for Vera. As I walked along the streets people pointed at me, "Look at Carolina!"

I spoke with some of them.

. . . I changed clothes to go visit the secretary of education. Dona Olga prepared lunch and left. (. . .) The kids returned from school.

. . . I took the bus. When I got downtown it was 3:30. I took a taxi to the São Paulo Academy of Letters, remembering the day the reporter and I went to take photographs and the doorkeeper turned us away. I hurried up to the eighth floor. The poet Eduardo de Oliveira was waiting for me in the company of some little black kids. They led me to a large room. I was waiting for the moment when I could speak to the secretary of education. He received us amiably. He is Dr. Luciano Vasconcelos de Carvalho. He told us he wants to create another kind of elementary school. He is a wonderful man. He's not haughty. He served us coffee.

February 22   I got up at 6 A.M. When I opened the door I saw Dona Olga sleeping. She's working for me. She got in late last night. I told her that I can't keep her because she goes out every day. I need somebody who can keep an eye on my kids when I travel.

. . . The kids went to school. I went walking around the market, looking at the astronomical prices. I bought some pillowcases, flowers, fish, and vegetables. (. . .) I wrote a note for João to take to the reporter. I gave him money to have two keys made. It rained while João was downtown.

João returned.

"The reporter is in Campinas. He went to interview Captain Henrique Galvão."

Captain Henrique Galvão is the Portuguese superman who defies and divulges [to the public] the dictatorial whims of Oliveira Salazar, the Nero of Portugal.

A woman came to ask me for help. She told me she went to the Social Services agency. She was crying. I could tell that she wasn't lying because I am familiar with the Social Services agency. The doctor gave her a prescription for gaining weight, advising her to eat meat, beans, and rice.

February 26 . . . I spent the day cleaning the house. Maria do Carmo came to invite Vera to go to the movies. In the afternoon I received visitors. A young woman named Aracy asked me to autograph a book. She wanted to see Vera, thinking it was cute that she didn't like to walk around barefooted. She commented on several passages in my book. (. . .) Some black people came to invite me to take part in the black festival in May and September.

. . . I thought it was interesting to hear what a black woman had to say. She said, "Carolina, you are able to pay for a maid. Get yourself a white maid, make her wear a little bonnet and an apron and have her scrub the floor. Make her scrub with steel wool, serve you coffee in bed and call you 'Dona Carolina.' Treat her like they treat us."

February 27 At 4 A.M. I began to read, and later I did some writing. . . . When I'm going to have breakfast I think back to when I was in the favela. In the mornings I would go ask the neighbors for some sugar and they would say, "I don't have any." My kids would go to school without having breakfast. When it rains I remember the scene in the favela: the kids walking barefooted through the puddles of water.

At daybreak I woke the kids up to go to school. I bought bread and cheese. The kids were happy and said, "It's good to have something to eat."

. . . I had a visit from a journalist accompanied by Sr. Waldemar Rocha, from Channel 9. The journalist who came to interview me is from Paraná. He is Sr. Jorge Barbosa Elias. He asked me questions for the newspaper *O Dia* in Paraná.

. . . I got ready to go out. (. . .) I took the bus and went to the Televisão Record studios. I arrived at 9 P.M. When I entered the radio station I saw the illustrious Sr. Durval de Sousa in the entrance hall. I met Sr. Souza Francisco. He told me I received the most votes on the program "Phone for the Best." I was going to receive a trophy. The first person to be interviewed was the father of Eder Jofre. He said that his son couldn't be there because he went to receive a trophy at the boxing academy. When I was interviewed I mentioned to the announcer Jota Silvestre that I intended to study. He gave me a statuette with the inscription "For Meritorious Achievement."

. . . After the program was over, I went outside to look for transportation. I walked down to the bus stop. I went in a bar at the invitation of a young black man who works at the [Televisão] Record studio. (. . .) I saw Eder Jofre's father get in a car. I got in the back, asking the driver to take me to Imirim. He said okay. We started talking about Eder again; he's a good guy. Eder's father told me he was an Argentine who had gotten married in Brazil and that he was by profession a boxing instructor. He had been a boxer when he was young.

At Eder's house his mother received me cheerfully. We had met previously. We met on the plane when I was returning from Rio. The house is a thing of beauty. As soon as I got out of the car the children recognized me and scattered. They went to tell their parents that I was in the home of Eder Jofre. I went to see the flowers adorning the back yard. The *dama da noite* flower was already in bloom. It's too bad that such a pretty flower dies so soon. I walked through the entire house, looking at everything and praising everything.

Dona Angelina Jofre gave me some candy. What delicious candy. Eder wasn't at home. I went to visit the home of Sr. Aristides Jofre's sister-in-law. It was supercrowded. (. . .) Eder arrived showing off his trophy, a gold medal. Eder's house is decorated with pictures of fights and trophies from boxing matches. One gets the impression that those trophies on display throughout the house are for the purpose of encouraging Eder in his boxing career.

I said goodbye to Eder, giving him a hug. The driver took me to my house. My kids were happy when they heard my voice.

March 1 I got up at 4 A.M. to write. What silence! The only voice is the sound of roosters greeting the new day.

. . . The sky is so beautiful. Clouds are dancing in the sky. Some of them are black, some of them are gray, and others are white. Everywhere there is a fusion of colors. Do the white clouds think they are superior to the black ones? If those clouds could come to earth they would be frightened hearing about the problems of social classes down here. Here on the earth, if a black person wants to impose his or her wishes he or she is killed. One can cite Patrice Lamumba.

I think I should be happy because I was born in Brazil where there is no racial hate. I know that the whites hold power. But they are human beings and the law is the same for everybody. If one could compare all the whites in the world, Brazilian whites would be the best.

Today I am happy. The sun is setting and night is falling. It is not raining.

. . . At 9:30 P.M. they arrived: Dona Edy Lima[36] and the cast of actors who will perform [a play based on] *Quarto de Despejo.* I welcomed them warmly. (. . .) I showed my house to my distinguished guests. I sang the songs I had written. They liked them. They ate the appetizers Dona Hilda had lovingly prepared. The reporter told me that I was invited to go to the inauguration of *O Ébano,* a newspaper for blacks. He told me I should go to the Paulista Teachers' Center to greet the blacks. I agreed.

. . . We got out of the car. (. . .) [But] when we arrived, the guests had already left. The black poet Eduardo de Oliveira amicably received us.

When I came back home João was showering. He told me he had been standing under it for two hours. It doesn't work anymore.

March 3 . . . There are times that I get annoyed and there are times that I am thankful for how my life has been transformed. There are different ways of changing one's life. There are rich who become poor and there are poor who become rich. For me, who used to eat from garbage cans, I should thank God for this change.

. . . The reporter told me that I should be at the legal office on Monday, to sign the papers making me the owner of my house. (. . .) I went to the bank to check if my balance was enough to pay for the deed. At the bank, they asked me how my book was doing.

"It's doing fine."

I told them I gave the bank's address to my foreign publishers so they can send me my royalty payments. The bank employees were cheerful. A woman employee wrote down my balance for me. I took [the slip] to the reporter who advised me not to withdraw money from the bank without consulting him. I got up and left without saying goodbye.

March 4 I got up at 6 A.M. because João was knocking at my door. I dressed the kids for school. They wear pajamas when they sleep.

. . . I took a shower and then I waited for Ivete to arrive so we could go to the Bela Vista Theater to watch the rehearsal of "Quarto de Despejo." I left the boys at home. Vera went to school. We took a taxi. I invited another woman to go with us. She got off at Tiradentes Avenue.

When we arrived at the theater I asked the doorman whether Dona Edy Lima was there or not.

"No, she isn't. But you can come in. The actors are rehearsing."

Dona Edy Lima arrived. We went to see the stage and the place where the audience would sit. We visited the rehearsal hall. The young man—who is going to be the lead actor—is handsome, tall, and intelligent. Some other young actors arrived. There is a *mulata* whose role is to be Fernanda. The director is young. He took us to a bar to have some coffee. I also saw the publicity photographs announcing opening night.

March 6 . . . I dressed João and I took him to school to talk to his teacher. She told me that he is not doing well in math. He feels too intimidated. I talked to the principal. He advised me to allow them to put him back a grade. The teacher told me that I should pay Cr$700 monthly to a teacher, a friend of hers, who would teach João in the afternoons.[37]

She gave me the math teacher's address.

I wonder what happens to a mother who cannot pay for a tutor.

. . . I gave Cr$1,000 to pay for this tutor. I came back home cursing the situation I was in. I was furious. (. . .) I complained about it to the reporter. I told him that I was taking João back to study in the countryside. The reporter listened to me in silence. Now, when he sees me he asks, "What's up?"

Each and every day I have something to complain about. I admire the reporter's patience when I am agitated. He understands my tension. I am the only one who works, who takes care of the house and the children, and who studies and writes. Right now I am involved with my public. I observe the different kinds of people and classify their characters. Some of them are corrupt people pretending to be honest. They are cynics. They have two faces. These people want to be part of high society but they don't belong. They dream about impossible things and they justify it by complaining, "If only I had enough money. . . ." I think they should say, instead, "If I had the guts to work. . . ."

These daily annoyances are making me nervous. There are days I can't even find time to write. (. . .) What I know is that my life is completely disorganized.

I am struggling to find my place in this "middle class" way of living. I just can't. My impressions fluctuate all the time. Some days I feel I am in heaven, some days I am in hell, and there are days that I feel like Cinderella.

March 9 I rose at 4 A.M. I did some reading. I am reading *Os Sertões* by Euclides da Cunha.

At dawn I began to get the children ready to go to school. João is being difficult. He doesn't want to be sent back to the third grade. José Carlos is a good boy. He doesn't miss a day of school. He says he wants to be a doctor.

I spent the day cleaning the house. I invited Hilda to go with me to the TV station. I put together the clothing that Ruth de Souza, the actress, is going to wear in the play "Quarto de Despejo." We left the house at 7 P.M.

When we arrived at the TV studio[38] the women who were going to take part in the panel were already seated.[39] I asked where the candidates' wives were because I only saw Dr. Farabulini Jr.'s wife there. (. . .) Dona Suzana Rodrigues reproached the candidates' wives who didn't show up.

. . . When the program ended I received a bouquet of flowers. Sr. Farabulini's mother-in-law invited me to her house. I invited the reporter. He refused and he told me that he had work to do. Hilda and I got there very quickly. What a house! It was a true palace. Hilda said, "Carolina, when you were living in a favela nobody would invite you to a place like this. It would be forbidden even to get into the house through the back door."

I was exhausted. I am fed up with having to be on display.

March 10 . . . I thought about my life's ups and downs after my book was published. My fame made people think that I am rich. Thus, goodbye to tranquillity. Everybody wants to be rich.

I met Dr. Lélio and Paulo Dantas at the bookstore and complained to them. People want the money I don't have. Some of them ask me for a million, or Cr\$800,000 or even Cr\$400,000. I am tired of hearing the word "money."

March 11 I got up feeling sad. João is giving them a hard time at school. He doesn't want to repeat third grade. I hired Dona Thelma to teach him math.

. . . I got dressed and I went downtown. The reporter was not there. I went to the bank to withdraw Cr\$20,000. (. . .) I got tired of waiting for the reporter. When I was ready to leave he arrived. He accompanied me to Barão de Itapetininga Street. We met a black youth named Osvaldo. He said he was the editor of the newspaper *O Ébano.* He asked the reporter to allow me to go with him to the newspaper building. The reporter told him I was free [to go wherever I wanted to].

I accompanied Osvaldo to the newspaper office. Osvaldo was nervous. A man telephoned and asked him to pay Cr$1,500 that was owed. They didn't have this amount of money and the man was going to sue them. I gave him Cr$2,000.

. . . We went for some coffee. I bought sandwiches for us. Six sandwiches for Cr$50 each. I realized that I had already spent Cr$2,300. Everywhere I go I have to spend money. I don't have anybody to help me earn that money. Well, I have the reporter. But he is methodical. He doesn't accept my money. I offered to give him half of my profits for editing my books but he didn't accept. [40]

Now that I have money everybody is after me as if I were a celebrity. I became the queen bee of a hive in which the bees want money, not honey.

. . . When I got home, what a mess! Plates and pans waiting to be washed, the floor dirty, beds waiting to be made, and the children unclean. I went to bed thinking that this was not the way living in a cinder-block house should be.

March 12 . . . I turned my eyes up to the sky. If I had wings I would take each one of my children to heaven and I would never return to earth again.

March 13 I got up at five and made breakfast for my children. They got dressed and headed to school. I am sad. I decided to clean the house. I washed clothes and cleaned the front yard. When I was going to start making lunch, Osvaldo, from *O Ébano,* came and invited me to go out. I became frantic. My God! I have children, I have to cook for them. I have a contract with the Francisco Alves Press, and Dr. Lélio doesn't bother me like Osvaldo does.

He said that our race needs to be united, that the ones who

are at the top have to help the ones at the bottom. He told me he was going to take me to Radio Record, to the Clube dos Artistas. [At least], this is what he promised. I got dressed and I left the house with him, against my will. I felt as if I were a leaf moving according to the direction of the wind.

. . . When we arrived at [Radio] Record we went to the restaurant. I sat at the same table where the artists [musicians and singers] were. I told them that I was afraid of writing a diary about my current life. The reporter told me I shouldn't fear it.

"So why doesn't the reporter write it?" suggested a young man I had never seen before.

. . . [Then] our show was announced. I headed toward the stage. We sat at small tables. Osvaldo told me he was going to launch me as a singer. He talked about *O Ébano.* I sang. I thought about my messy life. Today I am a singer. How about tomorrow?

March 15 . . . Each and every day there is a different thing to annoy me. Osvaldo came here and told me that I should sell my name and allow it to become a brand for bar soap "A." Then the profits could be used to publish the newspaper. He told me that [soccer hero] Pelé endorses any merchandise whose owners ask him. He said that our race needs to stand together.

. . . He succeeded in convincing me to collaborate with the newspaper. We went to see the owner of the bar soap "A." We didn't find him. He had left. His office is downtown, but his plant is in Guarulhos. We made an appointment for tomorrow. We headed to the office of Sr. Iram. We talked about *O Ébano.* He intends to print comic strips. Osvaldo told him that I could write stories in the newspaper. I told him I already had an interesting story. The title is "Where Are You, Happiness?" (. . .) Osvaldo told him that he was going to take me to Santos to take my picture with Pelé. He asked Dr. Iram if he could take us in his car. He agreed. I felt relieved when we took leave of each other.

March 16 . . . Osvaldo came to see me and to take me to sign the contract with bar soap "A"'s owner. (. . .) We headed downtown. Osvaldo was complaining about the many difficulties facing the newspaper, and he mentioned how much paper costs. Sr. Iram promised to help him. Osvaldo is full of prospects. Some enterprises need money, capital.

We went to the office of the owner of bar soap "A." He greeted us. After some unnecessary talk, they reached an agreement. I thought it was funny when the Portuguese man said to Osvaldo once the deal was made, "If you are in a hurry, there's the door."

Osvaldo became excited. I noticed that he is not a good businessman. (. . .) Osvaldo had no composure during the deal with the Portuguese man. They finally agreed and arranged to have the deal signed the next day. We left the office and went to *O Ébana.* The building was closed. We headed to the Casa da Imprensa. Cr$60,000 is needed to pay the printing bill.

March 17 . . . Osvaldo came here in a car. He told me he was going to take me to Santos and that he was going to photograph me with Pelé. I was still sleepy. (. . .) We went downtown to the office of *O Ébana.* Osvaldo told me that we needed to be back in São Paulo at 5 P.M. in order to sign the soap contract. (. . .) We went to Brigadeiro Luiz Antonio Avenue to check if Sr. Iram was going to go with us to Santos. He was not there. We headed on. The weather was cloudy and it looked like it was going to rain.

. . . I breathed a sigh of relief when we got to Santos. We headed to Pelé's house. He was not there. (. . .) We went to the soccer field to look for him. We met Coutinho.[41] He escorted us back to Pelé's home to check if he was still sleeping. He was not there. We could not wait for him. Osvaldo had me photographed giving Coutinho a copy of *Quarto de Despejo.* I autographed another copy for Pelé. (. . .) We said goodbye to the other players and headed back to São Paulo. When we got back we went to *O Ébana.* I gave Osvaldo money to pay for his gas.

We waited for the soap executive. We kept on waiting. Osvaldo was nervous. I told him to calm down. (. . .) We went to São João Avenue to look for a taxi. We didn't find one. We decided to walk to Frederico Abranches Street. I signed the contract in three copies. One copy was for the firm, the other for the agency, and the last one for me. The contract stated that I would permit my name to be used in advertising bar soap "A" and that the ads would appear in newspapers and on TV for a period of one year. They will pay Cr$94,000. Cr$60,000 goes to Osvaldo, for *O Ébano*, and Cr$34,000 goes to the owner of the agency.

Osvaldo told me that he is going to put my name on other products.

In the middle of all this "let's sell Carolina," I figured out that when I was at the favela I was worth zero. Now I have value. . . .

March 18 . . . Osvaldo told me that the newspaper was going to be distributed on Monday and he invited me to go to the Horto Florestal [Park] to greet Sr. Carvalho Pinto, São Paulo's governor. (. . .) I got dressed and we headed to Horto Florestal. At Sr. Carvalho Pinto's party there was lots of free food. There were sandwiches and sodas for the people. (. . .) I asked permission to go up to the speakers' platform. Osvaldo didn't want to go up because he wasn't wearing a tie. I saw the reporter and Torok up there. The reporter smiled and came over to me. I looked away. Today I'm upset with him. There is no special reason for it. He still helps me with everything I need. Thank God my life was improved because of this dignified man. He tolerates all my caprices with complete patience. Some days I am insolent. But it is not my fault.

. . . But let's come back to the governor's party. Several politicians were there. I walked around the park, looking at the people who came to pay homage to the governor and observing their outfits. There were descendants of Russians, Portuguese, and Japanese. It was a semi-Carnival party. People followed me asking me for autographs.

I thought the people dressed as Indians were interesting. There were Portuguese, blacks, and mulattoes among them. I smiled because I thought it was funny that these different races were wearing Indian outfits.

We left the Horto Florestal.

March 19   It is Sunday. I spent the day cleaning the house. I didn't receive anybody. I am feeling better. My children went to the movies.

March 21   Osvaldo from *O Ébano* newspaper came to visit me. He told me that the owner of bar soap "A" canceled the contract. He is going to sue him. He wants me to sign a writ. I told him that the reporter doesn't want me to advertise any kind of product.

He insists that it's my duty to help blacks.

I am confused. I have no inspiration to write.

March 24   Dona Didi is working for me [as a maid]. She wants to be paid Cr$7,000[42] monthly.

. . . I will have a dress made for my trip to Curitiba.[43]

March 25   I got up at 6 A.M. Today the children have no class. School buildings are being prepared [as voting places] for tomorrow's elections. I went to talk to Dona Elza Reis. She told me that Vera told her that José Carlos is stealing toys at the market. I became nervous. I put on my shoes and went downtown to talk to the reporter to find a new school for José Carlos. The reporter told me to transfer him to a full-day school in June. He told me he had deposited the money that had come from Holland. He gave me the bank receipt.

. . . Today nobody bothered me asking for money. I am going to bed. I need to sleep a lot.

March 26   I woke up early in the morning. Dona Didi is not coming to work. She is going to vote. I washed the clothes, cleaned the house, and prepared lunch for the children. They went to the movies. I am tired, but I am going to vote. I left with Vera. It began to rain. The streets were almost impassable, filled with water. I met two wretched children from the favela, Clóvis and Onofre. They looked curiously at me and asked, "Dona Carolina, where is João? Where is José Carlos?"

March 27   I went downtown. I am going to go with the reporter and Ruth de Souza. We are going to visit the favela. Ruth wants to see the people in order to be able to act on stage. We went to Ruth's place. She got dressed to leave. I thought it was interesting when she picked up the burlap sack that I used to scavenge for paper before getting in the car. I told her, "If scavenging for paper were like this, in a car listening to the radio, life would be a paradise."

Looking through the window I was reminded of the places where I used to work. When we got to the favela I felt concern for the poor people who inhabit such a filthy place. We got out of the car and walked towards the favela. Children could recognize me from a long distance.

"Look, it's Carolina!"

The favelados came out of their shacks to see me. They were barefoot and looked very dirty. Ruth was photographed near the water spigot carrying a can of water on her head. She was not perturbed by the situation. I was. Looking at that stream of water I thought of all the people who had to share it. It reminded me of the struggle it was just to fill up that can! I visited my old shack. I saw Dona Alice and she was sad. She is a seamstress. But she can't work because she doesn't have a sewing machine. Seu Chico was sleeping. The bed was dirty. This was not because of carelessness but because they couldn't afford to buy soap.

We went on our way inspecting the favela, São Paulo's shame.

March 29 . . . My front yard has a rose bush. Children pick flowers to play with them. I don't get mad because other flowers will flourish.

March 31 Today is Good Friday. I didn't buy fish. It was too expensive.

April 1 My children are out with other children making a Judas mannikin to be burned. They are saying that it represents [President] Jânio Quadros. I was horrified when I listened to the children crying loudly in the streets, "Let's burn Jânio!"

"The price of bread has gone up again. Let's burn Jânio!"

It makes me wonder: it has only been three months since he was elected.

April 5 . . . Dona A. asked me to lend her Cr$20,000. I told her to go talk to the reporter. (. . .) I went downtown. A woman recognized me on the street. She told me she saw me on TV in Rio and she wanted an autographed book from me. I invited her to go with me to the newspaper building. The reporter was there. I introduced him to the woman and told him he should give her a book. The reporter chided me, saying that I spend too much money. In my mind I cursed him: dog! skinflint! . . .

I left the place with the woman. I took her to Barão de Itapetininga Street. She was going to meet her husband there. During the ride I couldn't stop complaining because I am tired of the reporter's remarks. The woman said, "You are swimming in money; you have to spend it because things cost so much nowadays."

Her husband arrived. She let him see the book with my autograph. She told him about the reporter's reprimands, "It must be terrible to be his wife. . . ."

And her husband commented, "Poor Carolina. She is a vulnerable slum person with nobody to help her."

I listened in silence because she doesn't know the key place the reporter has occupied in my life. He is a buffer against people who want to fool me. I said goodbye to the couple and went to the bank to withdraw some money.

April 6 I got up at 5 A.M. I arranged my children's clothing because I am going to Curitiba. I ironed all their shirts so they won't have an excuse not to go to school. When Dona Didi arrived I had already washed the clothes and cleaned up the front yard. I went to the newspaper office to find out what time we would be leaving São Paulo.

April 7 I rose at 6 A.M. I got the children ready to go to school. I got dressed and I looked for my neighbor who is a taxi driver and who was going to drive me. (. . .) When we arrived at the airport the baggage handlers hugged me and said, "Our girlfriend is here."

They carried my luggage. The reporter and I entered the

airport lounge. We met Sr. Murilo Antunes Alves and his wife.
They were going to Brasília. He is going to be Sr. Jânio Quadros's
chief of protocol.

. . . As soon as I got into the plane I thought of my children.
Will Dona Didi take care of them as I would? We arrived in
Curitiba at II A.M. What beautiful pine trees! Journalist Jorge
Barbosa Elias was waiting for us. He is descended from a family
from Syria but he is concerned about Brazilian problems. We
talked to reporters from Radio Guayracá. (. . .) We headed to
the Lord Hotel. I changed my clothes and listened to the radio.
The people looked at the reporter and were impressed how young
he was.

. . . The reporter, Jorge, his father, Sr. Chafic Elias, and I had
lunch at Galeto Restaurant. What an agreeable person he is. The
radio was announcing our visit, "Carolina Maria de Jesus and her
discoverer have just arrived in Curitiba."

At 5 P.M. I went to the Do Povo Bookstore to autograph
books. (. . .) The journalist Ivar Feijó from *O Cruzeiro* magazine
was there. (. . .) At Radio Cultura we were part of a panel. The
questioners ranged from favelados to politicians. Sr. Vitor de Lara
asked me, "Why didn't you get married?"

I promised that I would answer him in my next book, *Casa de
Alvenaria*. Sr. Vitor de Lara from Curitiba, State of Paraná, this is
my answer. When I was young I dreamed youthful dreams. But all
the men who asked me to marry them disappointed me. Some of
them wanted me to steal for them, others wanted me to sell my
body to others. Men who asked me to marry them were not
worthwhile people. (. . .) I was horrified by their proposals and I
went on alone. Women's lives are filled with delusions about men.

Sr. Vitor de Lara referred to my children and told me that
they were bastards.

But they are happy children. I struggle for them and I have
never abandoned them. There are legitimate children who
envy mine. Those children have alcoholic parents who turn
their lives into hell. There are women who put their children in
orphanages because they are not able to fend for them. My
children don't miss a father. I am there for them.

. . . We had dinner at journalist Ivar Feijó's residence. Sr. Ivar Feijó's wife is very capricious. She gave me flower seeds. We went to TV Channel 12. The TV viewers called in questions by telephone.

April 8 I woke up at 5 A.M. I got up and opened the window. I looked up at Paraná's sky and then my eyes turned to the skyline of the gray city. I took a shower. I got dressed and went down to get my breakfast. (. . .) I asked the manager to get my luggage. I was feeling energetic. We went to TV Paranaense. I met the director, Sr. Nagib Chedi. The radio man Helcio José was there. (. . .) We said goodbye to the TV staff and we were driven to the airport. Jorge and I sat in the back seats. Helcio José was driving the car. He is a polyglot journalist. He has visited other continents.

When we arrived at the airport I became worried when I saw the airplane, which was shaped like a duck. I thought about my children and I asked God to look after me during the trip. We said goodbye to Jorge and Helcio José and headed toward the airplane. Before entering it I looked at the majestic scenery. The pine tree rises above the other trees like a leading theatrical figure.

We sat down and fastened our seat belts. The stewardess greeted us and wished us a good trip. I was seated next to the reporter. The airplane tried to take off, but the motor was not working well. I was frightened when the captain asked us to leave the airplane and to wait for a new announcement. I saw passengers leaving the airplane in a hurry. When I got out I looked at the open space and felt relieved. We went to the hangar. The passengers were agitated and were complaining, "If I had known I would have gone by bus."

The reporter walked around in the airport talking to Helcio José. I sat down, thinking about my children and about these hours going by. I was thanking God's intervention in not allowing the airplane to take off. Maybe God was protecting the reporter who was the best person of all on the airplane.

I thought it was funny that a honeymoon couple decided not to make the trip. I thought that they have so many plans. They are young.

I became happy when I heard them announce the time we would board. Most of the passengers had switched their flight to the last one of the afternoon. I met a disk jockey in his forties, he was very nice. When we were boarding I asked him, "Are you coming?"

"I'm taking an afternoon flight."

"Scaredy cat!"

He smiled at me. We went on. There were only half of the passengers. My heart felt like an eclipsed sun. It bounced inside my breast. I looked around saying goodbye to the pine trees of Paraná. The sky was cloudy. Paraná must be beautiful when the sun is out.

We entered the airplane. I froze looking at the reporter's watch. I thought about God and I wished I were in the favela.

Twenty minutes inside an airplane seemed like twenty centuries to me. (. . .) I looked at the reporter's watch. I was thinking that, oh my God, if the airplane falls and the reporter dies! Then I thought, oh my God, if the reporter dies I probably will die too because I am seated by his side.

I was frightened to death and I said to the reporter, "I decided to fly in this airplane because I wanted to show the other passengers that I am courageous."

He smiled at me and said, "You are paying too much for this caprice of yours. If I had known I would have changed your flight."

He calmed me down and told me that the captain would never depart if the airplane had a defect.

"He tested it three times before deciding to fly."

I felt relieved.

When I saw the "fasten seat belts" sign I smiled half-satisfied. I was impatient; I wanted to land. It was such a pleasure to see São Paulo's sky. The rainy sky that I love because it was under this sky that I suffered, struggled, and conquered.

At the airport I noticed that the people who worked there recognized me. They smiled at me. My heart was pacified.

April 9 Today is Sunday. Dona Didi came to work. She is vain. She wants me to buy expensive furniture, a [new] refrigerator. She says, "If I were you. . . ."

I bought the newspaper. I read [Adolf] Eichmann's statements, the Nazi executioner. I think that men are punishing the monsters of the last war while planning another one. Those who want war are irrational people.

April 10 My children went to school. I made their beds and washed clothes. It's a happy atmosphere.

Dona Didi arrived. I told her that she didn't do a good job preparing the meal.

"You forgot to salt the meat."

"Ah, I'm going to quit. I can't stand uneducated people."

And she left.

. . . I went downtown. We went to the publisher's. (. . .) I talked to Dona Adelia. She reproached me, "We were told that you are lending money. Don't do this. You gave Cr$6,000 to a woman. When you were living in a favela nobody gave you money. One of your neighbors tells us everything that is happening with you."

I didn't protest. I have gotten used to all these messy things in my life. I left the publisher's thinking about how someone is spying on me. Who is this person? Nobody can judge the way I live my life. I'm going to give Cr$6,000 to Dona E., a black woman. She is married. She has eight children and she can't count on her husband . . .

April 12 . . . Dona A. came to visit me. She asked me to lend her Cr$20,000. What a visit!

She told me that she has to pay a big debt. After listening to her I told her to go talk to the reporter. She promised me she would pay me back by working for me. (. . .) I went downtown. The reporter complained that I spend too much money. I felt unhappy.

April 13 . . . Dona A. came to work. We went to the newspaper building. I was happy and said to the reporter that I was going to take out Cr$20,000 for Dona A. He signed the withdrawal slip for me.[44] I said, "Now I have a white maid."

I withdrew the money from the bank. Dona A. came back with me and she was happy. (. . .) We went to the Bela Vista Theater.

We went by trolley. We got off at the theater. The actors were
rehearsing. I was warmly welcomed by the director of the play,
Amir Haddad. We decided that I would come back with my
children in the evening to watch the rehearsal of "Quarto de
Despejo."

. . . When I got home my children were playing. I told them to
get dressed to go to the theater. (. . .) When we arrived there were
some journalists. The actors were on stage. My children could
identify the scenes. João told me, "I get scared when I think about
that time in our lives."

We left before the end.

April 14 . . . Dona A. came to work. She finishes at 2 P.M. and she
leaves the dinner done. She was going downtown to pay her debts.
I gave her a message to give to the reporter. (. . .) He should come
see me at 6 P.M. to accompany me to the Otávio Mendes School.

. . . At 7 P.M. Norma's father and a student came to pick me
up to visit the school. (. . .) When we arrived there we saw the
students walking around. They led me to the main room. We went
to the stage. I sat and I thought about how my life has changed. A
very beautiful female student introduced me, telling them that she
had invited me to visit the school. I was eulogized by Edgard, a
student, and teachers Horácio de Carvalho, Wilson Pereira
Borges, and Benedito Vieira da Costa.

When they let me speak I said that I loved books. I told them
that I went to school only for two years but that since the day I
learned how to read I have been reading every day in my life. I
couldn't study anymore because I was poor. I told them that I was
earning more than Cr$500,000 per year. I was a winner who had
gone to school only two years.

. . . I was feeling happy among the students. Looking at the
young people, I thought that if there is going to be another war
. . . they are going to destroy the dreams of these young people.

April 15 . . . Vera went to school. She already knows how to read.
She says, "I want to learn fast because I want to read *Quarto de
Despejo.*"

April 17 . . . Dona A. came to work. I left when the masons who are going to work for me arrived. We went to the newspaper office. The reporter wrote a check for Cr$25,000 for me. I gave Cr$20,000 to the masons and I kept Cr$5,000 for me. The reporter told me to be careful with my money and with the friends I made after my life changed. He advised me not to give gifts. I went to the bank and took out the money for the masons. They promised me they would start working tomorrow.

I came back to the newspaper building. The reporter and I went to the Money Exchange to convert the money that came from Stock Publishers in France. Royalties from my authorship rights. I was touched by the idea of how my life has changed.

When we arrived at the Money Exchange we were very well received by the people there. The employees even offered us coffee. (. . .) After we left the Money Exchange we went to have lunch. How easy it is to get food nowadays. Before, I had to struggle so much to get something to eat. (. . .) After lunch we went to the Channel 5 studio. We met the actors who are going be in the play "Quarto de Despejo." Ruth de Souza, Celia Biar, and other actors were there. During the television show it was announced that the play is going to open on April 27.

April 18 My children went to school. The painters arrived. They will charge me Cr$39,200.

April 20 I spent the day at home. I will clean and take the clothing out of the closets and have them mended. A young woman from Jaú came here to visit me. She gave me a pin as a remembrance.

After my book was published several people have come here to visit me. I have become a tourist attraction.

April 21 The painters came here to start their work. Dona Luiza Fiori came here to visit me and to see my house. I showed her my dresses and sang some of my compositions. She fixed coffee. She admired my house but she told me it lacked a pantry, a garage, and a maid's room.

April 23 Today is Sunday. Dona A. came to work. She fixed our lunch and then went home to make lunch for her husband and children. She is sad, melancholy. Her biggest dream was to be rich but she is poor. This is the reason why she is in a disconsolate mood.

I will never understand human beings. The human being is the worst of all enigmas. Poor people want to become rich. Sick people want to become healthy. Fat people want to get thin. Single people want to get married. There are those who get married . . . and regret it. Those who are too tall or too short suffer from complexes. I met a black woman named Nair. She was disgusted because she was black. She didn't even go to the dances for blacks.

What a mess! Ah, I was talking about Dona A. She got married and she has four children. Her husband told her that he doesn't like living with her. That is why I don't have a good feeling about marriage.

I know I shouldn't say anything against it because I never got married. There are women who struggle to get married. She treats the man with velvet words. If her fiancé doesn't like short dresses she will wear long dresses. If he doesn't like makeup she won't use it. In short, the man's wishes prevail. After the marriage everything changes. She starts to use makeup and to get her dresses shorter because it is a new fashion. She leaves the house without telling him where she is going. She doesn't want children because they are too much bother. What I know is that most of the problems at home start because of the women.

I think it's beautiful when a couple commemorates their twenty-fifth wedding anniversary.

April 25 I spent the day at home. The painters are working here. I washed and ironed clothes. Days I spend at home make me feel content.

April 26 I hired cabinet makers to fix my closets. In the afternoon I went to the bank but it was closed. I came back home. The reporter has gone to Argentina.

April 27 . . . Dona A. arrived. I told her what to do. I went to the newspaper office to get a check for Cr$40,000 to pay for the work on the house. I was nervous because I knew the reporter would compare me to Marie Antoinette. I want my house to be beautiful. I am beginning to like my cinder-block house. It is a dream come true. The dream of a slum dweller is a cinder-block house.

I saw the newspapers. They were already announcing the play "Quarto de Despejo." I returned to the newspaper office. I met Sr. Mario Camarinha, the director of *O Cruzeiro* in São Paulo. He smiled and embraced me. I asked him to take my checkbook back to the reporter's desk.

As soon as I got home I gave Cr$15,000 to the workers to buy material. I talked to Sr. Abel about repairing the cabinets. I spent the rest of the day writing. I asked Dona A. to come back in the evening to take care of my children.

I am going out tonight. I will go to the opening of the play "Quarto de Despejo."

. . . The Bela Vista Theater was filled. There were important people because it was a benefit for charity. Well-dressed Paulistanos [residents of the city of São Paulo] were walking around the theater. (. . .) At the beginning of the show I went onstage to pick some numbers for a raffle. The people applauded. The play was pleasant. The most moving scene was the fight with the gypsy. During the scene, a pig that had been in a cage got out and walked around the stage. I heard somebody teasing, "This pig is an actor."

After the play ended I went to thank the actors. For me the performance was not complete because the reporter was not there.

April 28 Dona A. got my children ready to go to school. The painters arrived and then left to buy more paint to finish their job. I decided to make my back yard nicer. I am going to buy gutters for the house.

April 29 I got up early in the morning. The masons arrived one at a time. I went to the market and bought fruits and vegetables for

my children. (. . .) Some visitors arrived. I went to see who they
were. It was Dona Jurema and the writer Jorge Amado's wife.[45]
I was happy when I saw Dona Jurema Finamour. I remembered
the good days I had with her in Rio de Janeiro during the Book Fair.
I showed her my house. I introduced her to Dona A., "This is
the woman who works for me."

I showed her my dresses. Jorge Amado's wife took pictures of
me. (. . .)[46] I sang the songs I had written. They liked them. We
made an appointment to meet at the Claridge Hotel on Ninth of
July Avenue.

. . . When we arrived at the Claridge Hotel I called room 47.
Dona Jurema Finamour's husband answered it and asked me to
wait for him. I waited there. I am learning to wear high heels.
Sr. Lebret greeted me. We sat down. He told me that Dona Jurema
was not there but that Jorge Amado was coming to meet me. I
was excited. I was going to talk to Jorge Amado! I thought, God
willing!

Jorge Amado arrived. I got up and I greeted him. I hugged
him. (. . .) He speaks pleasantly. He gave me a book he wrote: *Os
Velhos Marinheiros* [*The Old Sailors*].

"How nice!" I said cheerfully.

I touched it gently and ran my fingers through the book.
When I looked at him I noticed that he was watching my
expressions. (. . .) Jorge Amado's wife arrived. I said "hi" to her.
She was looking at my dress. Dona Jurema Finamour entered. She
smiled at me. She looked at my dress and said, "How chic!"

. . . We left the hotel. We discussed where to go for dinner.
They decided to go to an Italian restaurant on Santo Antonio
Street. When we arrived at the restaurant, everybody stared at me.
I was very well dressed and I had Jorge Amado at my side. We
ordered baked lasagna. Sr. Lebret and Sr. Jorge Amado ordered
grilled chicken. They split the chicken with me. I wondered, What
if everybody could eat like this! We live in a period of time when
some people can eat whereas others cannot. (. . .) Bad times leave
a scar in our minds. There are moments when I remember, from
the favela, Dona Maria Preta's anguished voice, "I am hungry for a
small bit of meat."

I will never forget that hunger exists.

. . . When we left the restaurant we took two taxis to go to the Bela Vista Theater. I sat at Jorge Amado's side. I thought, My God, this is a dream. Yesterday I was a favelada. Now I am an ex-favelada. My life history could be summarized as follows:

Once upon a time there was a black woman who lived in hell. She escaped from hell and went to heaven.

. . . During the intermission people in the audience asked for my autograph. Jorge Amado and Dona Jurema Finamour went up on the stage to congratulate Ruth de Souza. Sr. Jorge Amado promised to visit me. My house is at his disposal.

. . . A journalist complimented me for the success of the play. (. . .) I came back home thinking about Jorge Amado. What a wonderful man! Instead of being named Jorge Amado [the one who is loved] he should have been called Jorge Amor [love]. (. . .) For me he is not Dr. Jorge Amado anymore. He is simply Jorge Amado. What belongs to the universe doesn't require conventions. We don't call the sun, Sr. Sun, or the moon, Dona Moon, or the wind, Sr. Wind.

May 1 What a lousy First of May. There were no civic exhibitions or parades of workers. The one who used to like the First of May was our esteemed Getúlio Vargas. Over the radio his voice traveled all over the country from north to south—*Trabalhadores do Brasil!* [Brazilian Workers!]

May 2 My children went to school. The masons arrived; they asked for more money to buy construction material to build a cover over the water tank. I went to the newspaper building. I met the reporter. Torok, the photographer, had stayed in Argentina.

. . . I left for Santos at 2. P.M. It was raining. I talked to a woman who was telling me, "You must be making a lot of money!"

I am sick of hearing this word "money."

May 3 Dona A. got my children dressed to go to school. I was still in bed but I couldn't sleep because the children were too noisy. I got up and went to buy a newspaper. It is raining. The masons are building the cover for the tank.

In the evening I went to the theater. It was the night dedicated to the critics. I remained seated, signing autographs and talking to the people. Women looked at me. The TV crew was there to film the event. They filmed me too. The actors were performing with great enthusiasm. I had the impression that it was another day at the favela. At the end of the play I went up on stage to thank the public. I sent kisses in return for their ovation. The TV cameras got shots of me next to Mauricio Nabuco, the main actor of the play "Quarto de Despejo." Dona Edy Lima got on stage and so did the director, Amir Haddad. The reporter didn't. I don't know why.

May 4 . . . I never thought that one day I would have a maid. The worst thing in all this is that Dona A. doesn't want me to mention her in my diary as my maid. She is always complaining about her bad luck.

May 5 I spent the whole day writing. The masons built the roof frame. In the afternoon I went to the newspaper building. (. . .) B. Lôbo, the music composer, was there. Also, Fernando Reis, the singer who is going to record a samba called "Quarto de Despejo." I thought it was funny when B. Lôbo said, "Audálio, since you are the one who protects the descendants of José do Patrocinio [a slave], you should sponsor this record for me."

The reporter promised him that he would. And I know better than anybody that his promises never fail. We arranged to go tomorrow to Silveira Sampaio's TV talk show. I came back home.

May 6 I spent the day at home taking care of my children's clothes. What a mess! My house is dirty because of all this construction work.

In the afternoon I got dressed to meet the reporter. We took a taxi and we got out at the Lord Hotel. We met Sr. Silveira Sampaio to plan the show. (. . .) We went to Channel 5. We met the people who were going to be interviewed. The first one to be interviewed on the program was Dr. Sergio Andrade, known as Arapuã from [the newspaper] *Ultima Hora.* He talked about his work and the origin of his nickname. After he heard the sound of an Arapuã bird he found it so beautiful that he adopted its name. I was the third one to be interviewed.

"Carolina, how do you feel being at the high point of your life?"

"I feel confused."

. . . Sr. Silveira Sampaio talked about my song compositions. (. . .) The interview went smoothly in a cordial atmosphere. When we left the TV station we went to have some coffee.

May 7 I went downtown to sign my contract with the Francisco Alves Press. The title of my new book will be *Casa de Alvenaria.* I read the contract very carefully. The publisher is going to handle the translations. The reporter told me that he is tired of taking care of it. The telephone rang. It was Dona Luiza Fiori, who had just arrived from Rio. She was at my house.

. . . I saw the magazine articles by Dona Eva Vastari from Finland. I said goodbye to the reporter. I was thinking that I need to buy two more blankets because Dona Luiza de Fiori is staying at my house. I went to a store run by friendly people. I bought two blankets, a jacket for me, and shoes for José Carlos. I spent Cr$7,000. This was the money for finishing the paintingin my house. I said this because I don't like to discuss money issues with the reporter. He is always complaining that I spend too much money. (. . .) I am tired of all his admonitions.

When I got home I found Vera combed and well dressed. She was being taken to school by Dona Luiza. She was wearing perfume. Dona Luiza knows how to dress a child.

May 8 I spent the day at home. Dona A. came to work. I sent João to the bookstore with a message to Dr. Lélio. I was asking for Cr$10,000 because I had to buy material to finish the construction work on my house. I complained in my message that the reporter thinks that I spend too much money and that I don't like his disapproval because I think it is unfair. It is terrible to have an owner like a slave. The Thirteenth of May [Abolition Day] is coming soon . . .

João came back and told me that Dr. Lélio was not there. I became nervous. The masons went away. Dona A. fixed lunch and left.

. . . In the afternoon Dona Maria José came to take me to church. We went to a mass celebrated at the request of blacks from the neighborhood. (. . .) When I arrived at the church I was welcomed by Father Constancio. What a calm man with such a serene countenance. They were waiting for me before starting the mass. That comforted my tired soul which is so skeptical about everything.

The church had some construction work still to be done. I loved the sermon and I thanked God that I am Brazilian and able to live without fears. We ought to love this country where there is no racial prejudice.

May 9   I spent the day at home. João didn't go to school. He went to the bookstore with the message asking Dr. Lélio for money to buy material. He gave me Cr$10,000.

I gave Cr$3,000 to the painters to buy supplies. A truck brought the material. Today I feel calm. I feel happy.

May 10   . . . The masons came to work. I intend to pay them quite well. We have to be honest in our dealings. I heard a commotion coming from outside. I went to look. Some children were playing with a balloon and the balloon entered a woman's house. I could count eleven children, but the woman was only cursing mine, "Irresponsible favelados, insignificant people. Doesn't your mother teach you anything?"

She doesn't understand that the favela is an invention of the rich. Poor people cannot pay the high rental prices. They cannot just live outside, either.

. . . Dona Maria José came to tell me that I must go to a party on the fourteenth. She gave me the invitation:

Don't miss the big benefit performance on 14 May to help finish the construction work on Nossa Senhora de Fátima do Imirim Church. There will be a show and a two-act play. We are counting on Carolina Maria de Jesus, the writer, to help us. Don't miss it!

Cast of the play "Despised Slave":

Master [Sinhô] Mauricio . . . . .Benedito
Master's wife [Sinhá] Jurema . . . . . . .Maria José
Foreman . . . . .Julião
Despised slave . . . . .Leontina
Princess Isabel . . . . .Irene Batista
Master's daughter [Sinhazinha] . . . .Sumoya Fuma
Maid . . . . .Ruth Rocha
Black Mathias . . . . .Clodoaldo
Father Inacio . . . . .Evaristo Gomes

Songs directed by Sabará. Choreography: José Garcia.

A young black man [came by and] asked me for help. He injured his right hand and cannot work. His nerves were severed and he lost the ability to move his arm. I asked him, "What about the law that protects workers?"

"They make it so difficult that in the end nothing happens."

"What do you know how to do?"

"I was a laborer. I did any kind of manual labor. Now I can't use my hands."

"If you were to run a newspaper stand you could earn a living. Pick a place and I'll help you get started."

. . . What could help resolve this young man's difficult situation would be the Labor Law. It is the insensitive employer who only values a man when he is able to produce. It is inhuman to abandon a worker injured in an accident. I bought the youth lunch [and then] gave him Cr$90.

May 11 I spent the day at home fixing things up. (. . .) I washed and ironed clothes. I don't have time to write because of the things I have to do in the house. Dona A. is embarrassed to be my maid because she is white. She arrives at nine and leaves at one.

May 12   I went with the painter, Sr. Ulisses Costa, to the office to ask the reporter for money to pay for the painting. Cr$34,500. I ran into Ramiro. I invited him to see the reporter. I introduced him as a person in my book.

When I quoted to the reporter how much I needed to pay the painters, he reproached me for spending so much. I cursed him mentally, "Dog! Wretch! You don't have control over the money I receive. . . ." He made out the check. I signed it. I took leave and went to the bank. We came back by bus. The reporter's disapproval saddened me. He gets his way because he was the one who helped me.

May 13   . . . I spent the day with the painters and the carpenters. I went to the Our Lady of Fatima store to buy wood to make shelves for the built-in closets. A black named Gazoza came to put up the rain gutter. The mason said that I should enlarge a room and put in a terrace. It would be a room for Vera. I want to fix up the house.

That night the directors of the Christian Union for Aid to Children visited. (. . .) I excused myself. I was going to change to go to the dance at Club 220, the club for blacks. They said goodbye and I went to change. Hilda came to help me with the dress I bought from Carmen for Cr$10,000. Hilda lent me gloves and a handbag. (. . .) I went to pick up Ivete at her house. When I walked down Imirim Street in my costume I noticed people staring at me as if I were from another planet. Ivete's mother was happy. Her cousins were there. They asked me, "Why don't you straighten your hair?"

"I don't like straight hair. I think natural is beautiful."

It was the first time I had gone into Ivete's house. It was her own, and well furnished. When I see a handsome house owned by blacks I feel content.

. . . Today is May 13, a sacred day for blacks who now live

tranquilly among whites. Today is a day when we blacks in Brazil should proclaim, "Long live the whites!"

We took a cab and went to the Bela Vista Theater. The reporter was at the door. By his look I could tell that he wasn't happy with my appearance. He doesn't know what the Thirteenth of May means to a black. It is a day of celebration for the Negro race.

. . . We caught a cab and sped away. (. . .) When we arrived at the Pinheiros Sport Club ballroom I saw several parked cars. What a marvelous club! We entered. Ivete's brother accompanied us.

The hall was lighted like a stage. In the back, uniformed musicians. Blacks and whites mixed together in fraternal festivity.

Sr. Frederico Penteado, the organizer of the dance, came to receive us. They paid homage to me: "The Year of Carolina Maria de Jesus."

May 14 . . . I worked all day. Ivete came to invite me to the theater at the church. I promised to go. In the evening Maria do Carmo came to get me. I went with the children. We encountered some youths playing drums. When they saw me, they shouted, "Look at Carolina!"

They started to sing. I thought it was nice. I gave a wide smile. At the church we went inside. (. . .) The people who were going to take part in the play were walking around, changing from their clothing into exotic costumes. The blacks wore trousers without shirts. Costumes symbolizing the past. I started the spectacle by reciting [my] poem "May Brides." I thanked them for the invitation to participate.

Some people were there who kept looking at me as if I were the Soviet [cosmonaut Yuri] Gagarin.

May 15 . . . I worked all day. At night I went to the newspaper offices to meet the reporter. We went to Channel 9. (. . .) I was interviewed by the councilwoman Dulce Salles Cunha. What a pretty woman! (. . .) I answered her questions calmly. I recited my poem "The Farm Worker and the Land Owner."

May 16 . . . The black fellow, Luiz Carlos Rocha, came to visit me.
He's been inactive since he injured his hand. He's afraid of glass.
He had four accidents with glass. When he sees a pane of glass he
gets frightened. He is educated. I praise him strongly because he
doesn't act as if he is incapacitated. I invite him to go out with me.

May 19 . . . I got up at 5 A.M. I got the children ready for school.
I started to prepare lunch. When I started lunch I thought of
the women in the favela. [Meal time is] The hour of pain. Of
gnashing teeth. (. . .) Poor people struggle with their difficulties.
. . . I went to the publisher's bookstore. I asked Dr. Lélio to
give me Cr$15,000. I hope the reporter won't come to chastise me.
  I complained to the brother of the reporter Thomaz Parrilho
that the reporter claims that I spend too much. I intend to finish
this diary, *Casa de Alvenaria,* and then go on [to perform on] the
radio. I like to be able to spend what I earn without being spied
upon.

May 20 I went shopping. I saw a school child badly dressed. I was
in the bakery and told him to wait for me so that I could tell him
where I lived.
  "When you get back from school come by my house and I'll
buy a pair of shoes for you."
  . . . When the child got out of school he came looking for me.
We went to buy the shoes. He looked at me and smiled. I paid
Cr$530. (. . .) He kissed me, saying "Thank you."
  I asked him, "Don't you need a *mãe preta* [black mother]?"[47]

May 21 . . . I need to go to the theater. (. . .) I left late and took
a cab. When I arrived at the theater it was 6 P.M. (. . .) I looked
around, observing all the well-fed and well-dressed people. The
word "hunger" is an abstraction for them. I sat down beside the
young Eduardo Suplicy Matarazzo. What an admirable youth! He
looked at the stage sets and asked, "But . . . is this how the favelas
actually are?"
  "Worse than this. This is a miniature version of what the favela
really is like."

A photographer asked me to sit next to Deputy Conceição Santamaria for a photograph.

When the play was over the actress Celia Biar came out on stage announcing the debate [scheduled to follow]. And she invited us to go on stage. And so we did. Solano Trindade, Conceição Santamaria, Professor Angelo Simões Arruda, Deputy Cid Franco, Dona Edy Lima, and I. Sr. Rogê Ferreira presided. He cited my book *Quarto de Despejo* as an accurate portrait of the hardships the poor encounter today.

I was confused to be in this group. I noticed that the high-society folks were embarrassed by the favela problem. It is a stain on the country. (. . .) The second speaker was Sr. Angelo Simões Arruda. He was reading *Quarto de Despejo* and making notes. He said that in São Paulo poor people work in factories and shops, not scavenging for paper. They do dignified work that provides for them a decent life.

I thought, If men in São Paulo had decent lives there wouldn't be any strikes for higher wages.

. . . Professor Angelo Simões Arruda went on, saying that indolent people do not find [decent] places to live; they live in the bowels of the earth.

[Talking about] bowels belongs in public bathrooms, I thought.

If the poor live on the banks of rivers it is because they receive no instruction, they don't learn how to do things. (. . .) Professor Angelo Simões Arruda did not mention the need to abolish the favelas, which are spreading rapidly throughout Brazil.

I was the third speaker. I said that I went to live in the favela out of necessity. As time passed I realized that I could get myself out of that place. It was horrifying for me to witness crude things that occur in favelas as if they were natural occurrences. (. . .) Favelados are the landless workers. Exploited by the land owners, they migrate from the countryside. They encounter hardship in the city because only people with good jobs find comfort and decency. Because of the high cost of living we are forced to scavenge in garbage or in the leavings of the outdoor markets.

"It's not worth talking about hunger with people who haven't experienced hunger."

When I wrote my diary I wasn't looking for publicity. But when I got home there was nothing to eat. I felt revulsion inside myself and started to write. I felt like I was spilling out my guts. That is how *Quarto de Despejo* was born.

I classified the favela as a "Garbage Room" because in 1948, when Dr. [Mayor] Prestes Maia began to urbanize the city of São Paulo, the poor people who had been living in the basements were thrown out.

The fourth to speak was the black poet Solano Trindade. He criticized Dona Edy Lima's script. He said that she didn't cite the hardships that my book relates, which testify to the extremely grave problem that the favelas represent throughout Brazil. (. . .) The public broke in, sometimes applauding, sometimes booing. Sr. Cavalheiro Lima, Dona Edy Lima's husband, defended his wife, saying that she did not alter the book. Her narrative kept the diary's simple language, displaying my caring for my children, my struggle to take them out of that awful place.

Solano Trindade pushed on, repeating what Ruth de Souza had said in the play: "When a child is hungry it is a problem for everyone."

I was horrified listening to hunger being debated before an audience. Deputy Cid Franco said that he had once been hungry, that he knew the hardships my book relates, and that capitalism is the cause of the division of classes into haves and have nots. Dona Conceição Santamaria said, "He is part of the capitalist system. He is undergoing a transformation in front of the public. He is holding hands with the capitalist system."

What confusion for me. I wanted to hear Deputy Cid Franco because of his culture. He isn't banal. He isn't a deal-making politician. He said, "If favelas exist it is because they are created and fed by the capitalist system, which sucks the life out of salaried workers."

"Untrue," said Dr. Paulo Suplicy.

A youth in the audience said that Deputy Cid Franco was

wrong blaming the capitalist system for social injustice. Deputy Cid Franco said, "My boy of eighteen doesn't fear the end of the capitalist system."

He was applauded. The students interrupted. I asked Deputy Rogê Ferreira to speak, because students are the men of tomorrow. The students booed the deputy. He sat down, saying that he never went to favelas looking for votes. He commented, "I don't reject the play. I reject the social system that favors a third of the population. I know that capitalism reneges on social reform."

"Yes!"

"No!"

. . . With all that confusion I thought I was back in the favela. Everyone speaking at the same time.

. . . The last to speak was Deputy Conceição. She started by saying that she helped the lepers. Because of her intervention the lepers are cured.

A voice from the audience, "We're not talking about politics. We're talking about favelas."

"Carolina said that there is much indolence in the favela," argued Dona Conceição.

"And in the Assembly," interjected a voice from the stage.

"In 1944, when I visited the favelas. . . . In those days the dictatorship was in power."

A voice from the audience: "You're pretty old, eh?"

Laughs.

Dona Conceição answered without becoming ruffled, "In those days they didn't have bad-mannered youths like you. I represent the majority, who voted for me. You speak for yourself."

A Japanese man spoke. A slow voice that was lost among the others. The rest were agitated. There was a sense that there would be a conflict in the theater. The students gave an ovation to Dona Conceição.

. . . When I left the theater I ran into the young Eduardo Matarazzo and said to him, "Did you notice the confusion in there?"

Dona Filomena Matarazzo invited me to have lunch at her house.

I took a taxi and went to my house.[48]

afterword: "a fish out of water"
by Robert M. Levine

To understand the relevance of *Casa de Alvenaria*, one must know the story of the first diary of Carolina Maria de Jesus, *Quarto de Despejo* (The garbage room). *Quarto de Despejo's* 182 pages describe in vivid detail the way its author survived by scavenging for trash. It refers not only to the garbage found in favelas, the shacks of the urban poor, but the name given to a back room in many Brazilian houses, an enclosed porch, or a space under the back stoop, used for storage of junk before its disposal. The title, then, refers to a nondescript place where castoffs and garbage were allowed to accumulate—just as human castoffs and people considered rubbish were allowed to accumulate in the growing shantytowns of Brazil's cities.

Quarto de Despejo sold ninety thousand copies within the first six months, making it the most successful book in Brazilian publishing history. It was translated into more than a dozen languages; the book is still in print in the United States, Canada, France, Great Britain, Japan, Germany, Cuba, and Russia. The U.S. translation, *Child of the Dark,* sold several hundred thousand copies in hardcover alone.

The foreign press embraced the book as an unprecedented glimpse into the life of an indigent woman from the Third World. *Newsweek* called Carolina's chronicle a "desperate, terrifying outcry from the slums of São Paulo . . . one of the most astonishing documents of the lower depths ever printed." The *New York Herald Tribune* called it "a haunting chronicle of hunger . . . a dramatic document of the dispossessed that both shocks and moves the reader." *Horizon's* reviewer said that the book contained "the seldom-told truth which inspires in some compassion, in some revulsion, and in others revolution."[1] *Life* magazine devoted a full page to Carolina; *Paris Match* ran a longer story. Novelist Alberto Moravia, in his introduction to the Italian translation of *Quarto de Despejo*, contrasted Brazil's natural beauty with the ugliness revealed by Carolina's diary, calling her the product of a "caste of pariahs" as damned as untouchables in India. In his prologue to the Casa de las Americas edition, translated as *La Favela*, Mario Trejo of Cuba called Carolina a conscience, a visionary, and the creator of a "subliterature rising out of the soil of underdevelopment."[2]

What message did Carolina's first diary convey? The entries span a long if disjointed period of time (July 1955, then May 1958 through January 1960), but they all fit the same pattern. In each entry Carolina describes in terse, colloquial language what she did from when she woke up to when she lay down to sleep. In this regard the reader comes away affected less by individual descriptions of suffering or poverty—although these are disturbing—than by a gathering sense of the numbness of Carolina's existence. Because the diary is so personal and so filled with detailed descriptions of her hour-to-hour activities, there is little explicit political content. Carolina in her diary did not advocate resistance to the system or revolutionary action because she was too tired after each day of scavenging.

Her overnight success brought about by the publication of her diary observations, first in the newspaper and then as a book, did not stop her from writing; indeed, her fame brought her closer to her lifelong goal of being a writer. She continued to write every day, even though now she was bothered by reporters and people seeking handouts, rather than drunken favelados. As soon as the first diary began to sell wildly, Carolina's publishers decided to issue a second one, titled *Casa de Alvenaria,* literally "cinder-block house." The cinder-block house was a long-held dream for Carolina, which she achieved after her incredible stroke of fortune. Her discovery brought her enough income to allow her to escape the cursed favela.

Audálio Dantas, the journalist who discovered her and who wrote the preface to *Quarto de Despejo,* penned a very different kind of introduction to *Casa de Alvenaria.* He starts,

> [This book] has the same format as the diary written in Canindé favela; in essence, however, it is very different. It is testimony, as well, but about another world—the

cinder-block world she longed for and attained. [It] is
testimony as important as *Quarto de Despejo*, even without the
dramatic tone of favela misery. In certain ways it is a more
fascinating book because in it there is a bit of happiness,
the sense of awakening discovery, the satisfaction of a filled
stomach, the perplexity about things and people who are
different, and a bitter fact: misery also exists in the cinder-
block world, in different forms.

Starting with an event that well may have been the most
important in her life—the signing of the contract to publish *Quarto de Despejo*—Carolina narrates the day-to-day
rhythm of her new life, but this narrative assumes a new
dimension; they are no longer always the same, dogged
by hunger. The surprises, the shocks, and great joys follow one after another in this register that contains both
human interest and value as a sociological study.

The condition of the people who travel through these
pages in almost all cases differs considerably from that
of those anguished souls from the favela world of boards
and zinc sheets. Here they are seen, many times with de-
formities, by a creature who always lived on the margins,
a *socially dysfunctional* person who fought desperately to enter
the larger and less unhappy world of society's living room.
Just as from her "garbage room," she continued to write
her diary and reveal herself. But the new portrait has some
distortions, some functioning as a glass of perfect clarity,
others cloudy. But *Casa* is a portrait. It contains within it
the artist's contradictions, and, above all, the contradictions of those it depicts. Not always do Carolina's insights
reflect things as they are, but that is not her obligation.
She attempts to *focus* her lens, with her acute sense of observation, but she does not attain the necessary depth.[3]

Dantas, with whom Carolina always had a stormy relationship
and from whom she irrevocably drifted apart after the publication
of her second diary, understood how difficult it would be for Carolina to live in her new environment. Unfortunately neither Dan-

tas nor anyone else from that world reached out to help Carolina emotionally after she became comfortable financially. Carolina's tragedy was that although foreigners continued to honor her as an emblematic figure, to Brazilians she quickly became passé. No one seemed to understand how difficult her transition would be to the middle-class world of solid houses, nor did anyone seem to care as she floundered in that world. Her second diary offers fascinating insight into Carolina's journey from one kind of despair into another.

Historical Background

Ill-prepared for her meteoric rise to fame after her diary was published, Carolina Maria de Jesus went from being a woman reviled for her blackness, her illegitimacy, and her poverty to a woman mocked for her supposed ingratitude and lack of docility. Few attempted to understand her. Brazilian feminists, who mostly wrote against their mistreatment by men, never took her as a heroine. Intellectuals ignored her painful, extraordinarily detailed autobiographical writings, so revealing about her childhood and her strategies of coping with extreme hardship. They ignored the abuse hurled at her because of her expression of her sexuality. She was not alone; she was, in fact, one of legions of destitute Brazilian *mulheres sós*, women "on their own," not legally married, who could not look to anyone for support.[4] She died a broken woman, forgotten in Brazil, her miseries only fractionally relieved, her remarkable life overlooked. She had lived independently with a self-sufficiency that was often misunderstood, but she never really found her way. Her greatest wish was to be accepted as a writer, but even this eluded her and left her bitter. She stubbornly refused to accept what was considered to be the role of the poor, and especially poor black women—to suffer in silence.[5] Many rejected her because once she became prominent, her behavior seemed "common" and "ordinary." In a society like Brazil's, where being "ordinary" is not admired, few were able to recognize that she was, in fact, an extraordinary human being.

Following the enormous success of *Quarto de Despejo*, Editora Francisco Alves contrived a series of books on popular themes, designating Carolina's first diary as "Volume I." The second book in the series, a nondescript homage to the turn-of-the-century author Euclydes da Cunha, went nowhere, as did the third, *I am Pelé*, a ghost-written autobiography of the soccer star Edson Arantes do Nascimento. *Casa de Alvenaria* was designated as the fourth volume in the series. Although the book sold modestly well, the series ended with its publication. *Casa de Alvenaria* received little attention and was soon forgotten.

Dantas, Carolina, and the Editing Process

Audálio Dantas titled his six-page preface to *Casa de Alvenaria* "The Story of a Social Ascent." He begins by reminding his readers how he discovered "a black woman named Carolina Maria de Jesus" in April 1958 in Canindé favela in São Paulo. The first diary's entries, he said, constituted a "revolution"; later on in the preface he calls Carolina's words "subversive," although he argues that the problem in the second diary is not the misery of hunger but other kinds of misery, by-products of Carolina's education about life. This emphasis is ironic, since Carolina never considered herself a social critic; nor did she want to be known as a diarist. Dantas knew, however, that her market value came from this, and he pushed her to cultivate this side of her talent.

Foreigners reacted to Carolina in this way, although most Brazilians did not. The *New York Times* called *Quarto de Despejo* "an immensely disturbing study of what can happen to a segment of the population in one of the world's potentially wealthiest nations" and "an extraordinary sociological document."[6] Dantas had considered her writing incendiary, the words of "a marginalized woman who fought desperately to gain entry into a larger and less unhappy society."[7] But it is telling that neither Dantas nor very many of the other Brazilian reporters and social critics who found in Carolina a "revolutionary" writer ever bothered to pursue this theme. Carolina became a national and international celebrity, but despite a torrent of publicity, interviews, articles, and television programs in Brazil, hardly anything was done about the social issues that Carolina wrote about.

In his preface Dantas acknowledges Carolina's "astute sense of observation" but he fails to mention any specific instance where her insights about social injustice were worth considering. In fact, the diary's social commentary was the key to its great success abroad, but in Brazil her comments were taken by many to be embarrassing, even considering that the early 1960s were unprecedented years for reformist ideas. The sad fact about both of Carolina's published diaries is that they had precious little impact on the way that Brazilian society dealt with severe poverty.

The reporter appropriates Carolina's metaphor about where she lives to suggest that she should have been satisfied leaving the "garbage room" of the favela for the "cinder-block [suburban] house" of her dreams. In the favela, she had nothing, he writes; now, a year later, she has received Cr$250,000 [$1,325] in royalties and has moved into a small house with a living room, a parlor, two bedrooms, a kitchen, a patio, and a garden with a rose bush. The rest of his preface, however, explains why this was not enough for Carolina, who was, in his words, "now inebriated with success" and her own worst enemy. He chides her for ignoring his advice not to squander her money or to fall for schemes in which others sought to exploit her. She had tunnel vision, he suggests: for Carolina everyone who lives outside of favelas is "rich." She is a "fish out of water." He reminds us that at one point, realizing that fame was deceitful and would not bring happiness, she was so confused that she wanted to move back into the favela.

Neither Dantas nor the other critics who gave up on Carolina after the publication of her second diary were willing to take seriously the observation that Carolina herself made in her second diary on 3 December 1960, relating a conversation that took place when she dined with her translator, David St. Clair, in an elegant Copacabana restaurant during her promotional tour of Brazil. "The women who were at my table spoke about social reform," she says. "I thought, They are philanthropists in word only. They talk big, but it's just talk. Chattering parrots. It's only when they see me that they remember there are favelas in Brazil." Dantas's preface criticizes Carolina, reminding his readers of her "quaintness," and he claims that not only Carolina but the majority of her fellow favela residents from Canindé "now live in cinder-block houses." This is a dubious assertion despite the extremely brief flurry of steps taken by city authorities to help favelados after the success of *Quarto de Despejo* a year earlier, in 1960.

In his preface, Dantas categorically denies having put words into Carolina's mouth. Some critics in Brazil from the outset doubted that an indigent black woman living in a favela could have written what was attributed to her—a calumny that is still held in Brazil by those who should know better, including the otherwise distinguished literary critic Wilson Martins, who on the occasion of the reissue of *Quarto de Despejo* in 1993 called the diary a "literary hoax" in his nationally syndicated column. "I kept the author's language and grammar without altering it in any way," Dantas stated in response. "In the work of compilation there are long cuts, but without significance. The essential, the important, remained. . . . What I did was something similar to editing a film. The originals are preserved lest anyone challenges me," he concludes. [8]

Dantas's 1961 preface to *Casa de Alvenaria* concludes with an oddly patronizing injunction addressed personally to Carolina, rejecting her efforts to be a writer, something she prized more than any other goal after providing for her children. "Preserve your humility," he wrote, "or, better, recuperate the humility of which you have lost a little—not by your fault—in the dazzling lights of the city. Save your 'poems' those 'stories,' and those 'novels' that you have written. The truth is that what you shouted is very strong, stronger than you can imagine. Carolina, ex-favelada of Canindé, you were my sister there and you are my sister here as well."

Carolina's archive shows that he is telling the truth: Carolina's words were her own. Dantas simply edited them, making cuts. Over the years, however, he has refused to allow anyone to see the entries from the first diary, which he has in his possession,—and which would ostensibly prove his case. Vera Eunice de Jesus Lima, Carolina's surviving daughter, has enough examples of her mother's original diary entries to lay to rest definitively any doubt that her mother wrote everything that was published under her name.

In 1995, José Carlos Sebe Bom Meihy and I convinced the Rio de Janeiro office of the U.S. Library of Congress to microfilm Carolina's entire archive, which was rapidly falling apart from age and humidity. This seemed to be a good solution—earlier efforts to have a Brazilian institution agree to house the documents came to naught, but now copies of the microfilm are being deposited in the Brazilian National Library, which is using its equipment to do the microfilming. Examination of this treasure of personal materials, including two unpublished novels, short stories, hundreds of poems, and many of Carolina's handwritten diary entries, confirms that what Dantas said is true. Yet, paring down Carolina's thousands of diary entries to two short edited volumes—*Quarto de Despejo* and *Casa de Alvenaria*—depicted Carolina in a limited kind of way, in contrast to the more rounded impression that would have come through had all of her diary entries been published. But Dantas never put words in Carolina's mouth, as some Brazilian critics over the years have alleged.

Both of Carolina's published diaries provide a clear roadmap to Dantas's editing. The text contains (. . .) notations, contrasting with . . ., Carolina's own device for showing the passage of time. It is telling, moreover, where the (. . .) notations occur. More often than not, Dantas removed material directly following a disparaging statement by Carolina about one subject or another, or, in several places, a clash between the two. Dantas also seems to have edited sections out of the diary when he thought they would be controversial: when Carolina's son José Carlos, for example, arranges for a white woman to work for them as a servant. Dantas likely did not want Carolina to explain fully her complaints against him in their stormy and complicated relationship. Dantas's practice of abridging or deleting controversial portions of the diary suggests further that although Dantas did not write words for Carolina, he believed that he had the right to censor her. He believed that he did this for her protection: after all, Carolina, as an indigent lacking proper papers, was not even allowed by Brazilian law to have a bank account under her own name. Every time she wanted to withdraw part of her royalty money or have a check signed she had to take a bus to downtown São Paulo to the newspaper office where Dantas worked to have him sign it.

At one point early in her diary, Carolina begins to refer to him as "the reporter," not as "Audálio" or even "Dantas." Her diary, in fact, presents a dialogue between Carolina and her benefactor. Sometimes she acts exactly as if she were married to him, as if he were a dominant husband. She becomes angry at him because he has a habit of arriving late and scolds her for spending too much money. Ambivalence colors her moods. Elsewhere she describes how she suppresses her anger, cursing him silently but holding in her feelings because "he helped me." The diary entries waver between castigating Dantas and seeking his approval. At one point she says that she "puts him on a pedestal" out of gratitude for his rescuing her from misery. She also curses him under her breath, sometimes openly. In later years Dantas mocked Carolina's belief that the Chilean university professor Jorge Mendoza Enriquez had promised to come to visit her in Brazil, saying that "no real professor" would ever do this. Mendoza never did come, a fact that crushed Carolina's spirit and further estranged her from Dantas. Dantas also felt betrayed by her when she acted against his advice (about paying to have her samba recorded, for example). Dantas lost touch with her after she sold her house in 1970 and moved to distant Parelheiros.

The Second Diary

Although *Quarto de Despejo* brought its author international acclaim, *Casa de Alvenaria* sold modestly and had virtually no impact in Brazil. Carolina's diary entries follow the same pattern as before, starting with her rising in the morning and commenting on the activities of her day. As before, she details selected events in her life from the seemingly mundane to the extraordinary (for example, telling in detail how she and her children were stoned when they moved out of the favela). Once again she writes in colloquial Brazilian Portuguese, the language of the street, not the flowery rhetoric of literary language.[9] In *Casa de Alvenaria*, Carolina explains at great length her stormy relationship with her discoverer: sometimes she reviles him for being a Svengali; other times she acknowledges her debt to him. On the whole, however, she becomes increasingly testy about him and is angered when someone else points out that he should have removed her from the favela months before she actually was able to leave.

Written at a new point in Carolina's life, *Casa de Alvenaria*, of course, is a very different book from its predecessor. Hunger is no longer the constant theme, although Carolina frequently comments on the sufferings of other poor people. Instead, the second diary is a psychological portrait of the dizzying effects of sudden celebrity, of the small and large shocks experienced by a woman, once a scavenger, now a guest at governors' mansions, media interviews, and book signings across Brazil. This diary is the story of a human being transported to another world; Carolina not only had never traveled by plane before but crammed food into her mouth with her fingers at literary society luncheons. People constantly stared at her, as if she were a strange creature. Her diary entries frequently cite examples of how she does not fit in, despite her fame.

Nevertheless, Carolina views her success as a reward for her hard work and her lifelong dedication to writing. At the same time, feelings of guilt surface; when she eats in a restaurant her thoughts drift to her brothers and sisters in poverty. She yearns to demonstrate her erudition: she repeats the full name (and title) of people she meets; she gives the addresses of banks and bookstores and offices she visits, as if anxious to show that she was no longer a nameless person in a nameless place. In a tone many found annoying, she comments on world figures and international events. For example, she speaks of her greatest hero, John F. Kennedy, whom she saw as a champion of civil rights for blacks; the execution of the convicted murderer Caryl Chessman in the United States (she opposes capital punishment); Fidel Castro (she says she adores him for freeing his country); and the slain African leader Patrice Lamumba. She protests against the deprivations caused by war, which she hates, and the problems caused by money, about which she displays mixed feelings.

Three and a half months after Carolina signed her book contract with Livraria Francisco Alves, she received an offer from a compassionate man of Portuguese descent, Antonio Soeiro Cabral, to rent a room in the back of his house until she could find a house for herself. Her departure from the favela—even though her neighbors stoned her and her children when they moved out—fulfills her wildest dreams, and, briefly, her spirits soar. She attributes her success to hard work, to her dedication to her writing, and to the fact that she sacrificed to educate herself. Reality, however, soon asserts itself. She notices that her new house is dirty—the previous occupants neither removed their possessions nor cleaned it—and flea-infested. She begins to feel guilty, especially when she sees poor people. "I have the impression that I escaped from the sea but left my brothers and sisters to drown," she writes. Her family, with their rough favela manners, does not fit into the new neighborhood. She soon realizes that money brings not only stability and release from hunger but also constant harassment from opportunists and difficult decisions, which she has not learned to make. She expresses amazement that people can debate the topic of hunger without having experienced it.

The second diary recounts Carolina's journey out of obscurity into the harsh light of celebrity. To a man who tells her that she "came out of hell and now is in heaven" she retorts that he's mistaken; she's in purgatory. Still, her early entries are filled with wonder and optimism. "What fascinated me was the cultured ways of the hotel employees," she muses when she is taken with her children to the august Hotel Serrador. "It made me feel like I was in heaven." She expresses horror at the amount of food restaurants throw away. She tells her diary that her new world is sublime, "without confusions." Quickly, however, reality intrudes. Disappointments plague her, and she begins to retreat behind a wall of ironic observations, no longer trusting and cheerful as she was in the first days of her fame.

Her second diary's Portuguese title, meaning "cinder-block house," was aptly chosen. Carolina reminds herself repeatedly that having a real house was the culmination of her lifelong dream, but she also understands that the torment that accompanied her fame exacted a very high price. Her diary recounts her efforts to repair the house (every time she needed to pay workmen she had to go to Dantas for a check), to keep it in good order, and to receive the steady stream of visitors who ranged from reporters to curiosity seekers to needy people asking for handouts. She wants to be left in peace. When she does not have to put on her shoes and go out to sign books, or to have Dantas write a check for her, she is happiest in her little house. There she writes, or she reads serious books such as Euclydes da Cunha's *Os Sertões*. For this, people mock her for putting on airs, just as they did when she was a girl growing up in rural Minas Gerais.

Of very dark skin—a *negra retinta* as Brazilians called her, referring to her African appearance—she experienced constant prejudice.[10] When the neighborhood children squabble, her children are always singled out as "those favela brats," especially by descendants of Italians. Dona Didi, whom she hires as a maid, quits when Carolina finds fault with her; the woman replies that she "can't stand uneducated people" and quits. Some people treat her patronizingly; others attack her with invective, angry at her fame. She gives the impression that she is never really welcome, and she frequently cuts short visits because, after the initial thrill of being recognized as a famous person, she soon tires of all the commotion. When she is on her publicity tour she worries that people will think her a "Red" because of her "radical" political ideas, which in fact are not so radical. She overhears a man calling her "an ugly black woman." She experiences confusion over restaurant menus. At one point she admits that she is losing courage to write more diary entries because the turmoil of the lives around her is too depressing.

She is handicapped by the cultural disadvantages she carries with her. She habitually reports how much things cost, from taxi fares to repairs on her new house—because she remains astonished at having money. She does not know which days are work holidays, for example, so sometimes she is unable to buy things she needs because she finds the stores closed. Educated people continue to say cruel things to her. José Roberto Penna, a reporter, calls her "semiliterate." Carolina knows that she is quite literate but she understands that the epithet also calls her uncultured, something that stings, since all of her efforts to be understood and accepted as a normal person fail. She learns, too, that she cannot control her children in spite of her tenacity. She never saw her youngest son—José Carlos, who wanted to be a doctor, and who never missed a day of school—achieve the stability she wanted for him. Ironically, she was a teetotaler but as an adult José Carlos became an alcoholic, unable to hold a job or support his children.

Not that Carolina was always candid in her diary. We know that she protested when the theater producers who staged *Quarto de Despejo* cast a professional actress, Ruth de Souza, as Carolina when Carolina really wanted to play the role herself. Her diary tells about Ruth de Souza's visit to the favela and about Carolina's participation in the opening-night ceremonies at the theater but never admits how bitter she actually felt.

The diary is revealing about Carolina's attitudes toward charity. Generous to a fault—she constantly tells how Dantas warns her to be careful with money, although her diary reveals that she gave it away freely in part because she was moved by the genuine stories of hardship that supplicants told to her. She also gave gifts so that people would not bother her anymore, or because she thought she would win their esteem. Often Carolina shows that she is trying to buy social acceptance. People sense this, and they take advantage of her. The black journalist Osvaldo, eager to use her name to raise funds for the newspaper *O Ébano*, not only takes a large subsidy from her but takes her around the city with him trying to sell her commercial endorsement for soap products. Carolina senses that she is being used but she goes along. Although Brazilians considered her uppity and devoid of manners, she lacked the inner strength to say "no" to people, and in the end this trait accelerated her descent into poverty after her Brazilian royalties stopped coming. The diary also recounts the delicious irony of the fact that Carolina's second maid is white, a woman who had borrowed money from Carolina and who, unable to repay the loan, had agreed to work for her. Not that the relationship is a good one: Carolina tells her diary that "Dona A." feels shame having to work for her and hints that the maid takes advantage of her.

As the diary entries wind down, Carolina clearly indicates that her Cinderella role has so exhausted her that she decides to disengage herself from her beloved "cinder-block house" existence. Her final entry is an insightful description of a tumultuous public debate on poverty and favelas in which she mocks the pomposity of some of her fellow speakers. Normally Carolina skims the surface when she describes events like these, always maintaining her distance as if she were the person from another planet she feels that others see her as. This time, though, she writes like a journalist, with accuracy, engagement, and wit. But she also reveals her weariness. The wealthy Dona Filomena Matarazzo Suplicy invites her to lunch, but Carolina simply ends her diary with a cryptic comment that she took a taxi home. This indifference prepares us for what happened later: she soon would sell her precious house and move far away as a recluse. In all, the second diary documents what Carolina termed "making concrete my dream." But danger signs pervade her daily life. In an eerie foreshadowing of her ultimate return to poverty, she reveals her fear that the prosperity she now enjoys will be short-lived: "I feel like I am really just iron covered with a layer of gold. And one day the gold leaf is going to fade and I will return to my natural state—iron."

Her diary is important not only for what it reveals about Carolina's life after she became famous but also for the details it offers about Brazilian society. Carolina describes mundane things about daily life that readers might not otherwise realize. She meets a woman named Nair who was so depressed at being black that she does not go to "dances for blacks," a reference to the entirely segregated lives of blacks and whites in her country and especially in the city of São Paulo. Carolina quietly hopes for racial harmony. When she sees whites and blacks together she comments on how good this makes her feel. She is glad when she visits her black friend Ivete and finds that she lives in a house that is comfortable and well furnished. Her comments about her disappointment in the lack of traditional May Day commemorations in 1961 and her cogent observations about the black youth who loses use of his hand in an industrial accident but for whom Getúlio Vargas's labor legislation has done nothing reveal much about the legacy of Vargas. She loved Vargas, who committed suicide before he was to be ousted as president in 1954, for his populist rhetoric in behalf of ordinary Brazilians.

The diary discloses what money meant to Carolina. She considered herself rich when she was handed her first royalty check for $212, the equivalent of slightly more than a thousand dollars today. She and her children felt amazement at having 1,000-cruzeiro bills in her purse. On her earnings she was able to have a maid, who demanded a higher wage because she had to work for a black, former shantytown dweller.

She lists the royalties from her first diary, *Quarto de Despejo,* that Dantas deposited for her in her bank account, enough for her to purchase her little cinder-block house. Royalties for *Casa de Alvenaria,* however, were much less, since the book did not make nearly the same commotion as the first. Carolina earned very little in foreign royalties over the years—mainly from the United States and from France—because her publisher sold the translation rights to her diary, never guessing that Carolina would become an international sensation.

Carolina's published books sold in many countries for decades, but only enough money came in before her death to sustain her existence as a recluse, and it did not provide enough money to bury her.

Carolina in Argentina, Uruguay, and Chile

Casa de Alvenaria was translated into Spanish in an Argentine edition but never appeared in English, unlike *Quarto de Despejo*, which, titled *Child of the Dark*, sold more than 350,000 copies in the United States alone. The second diary traces Carolina's good fortune, from the decision of Livraria Francisco Alves, one of Brazil's most prestigious firms, to publish her diary as a book through the heady days of her fame and her move with her three children to a cinder-block house, a *casa de alvenaria*. The Argentine edition is important because it contains an extensive appendix of diary entries from her trips to Uruguay, Argentina, and Chile, entries that never were published in Brazil.[11] Not only are the entries revealing, but the way the translation was packaged for publication in Argentina is telling in itself. For one thing, the Spanish title, *Casa de ladrillos* (brick house), was an inaccurate translation. Carolina's dreams were more modest. She craved only a small cinder-block house, accessible to relatively poor people. Brick houses, which required much more craftsmanship, were reserved for the very rich. For another thing, there are fewer (. . .) ellipses in the appendix text. The nameless Argentine editor, for whatever reason, seems to have made far fewer cuts than Dantas. The first diary entry in the appendix is for 15 November 1961, the day of Carolina's departure by plane for Argentina. *Casa de Alvenaria* had not been published yet; the publicity tour was because of her first diary. She described the drudgery of having to get up at 4 A.M. in the rain to go to the airport, but she could not hide her excitement. "Argentina is supposed to be very pretty," she told herself. An Argentine man at the airport asked her if she was going to bring her chicken-feather dress that she painstakingly made for Carnival and in which she has been photographed. She also felt self-doubt, a freak. "I have the impression that I have become transformed into a [media] phenomenon," she wrote, "only because I know how to write."[12]

As soon as she departed Brazil, however, Carolina became less

self-conscious, more willing to criticize. In Brazil her driving personality was always tempered with shy reticence, a fear likely carried
since her traumatized childhood. She spoke out more and the tenor
of her diary entries changed. Sometimes she seemed relaxed; at other
times she showed petulance. She learned that a fellow passenger was
an economist and wrote in her diary, "What kind of economics can
you teach to peasants if their income is so miserable?" People sitting
near her told her to write more, to enlighten the public.

Foreigners asked her more pointed questions than did Brazilians: "Why are there so many favelas in Brazil?" she was asked on
the airplane. Her answers advocated reform, changes in attitudes,
more resources for the poor, better government. It is ironic that
Carolina expressed fewer of these sentiments in Brazil. One of the
reasons Brazilian social democrats rejected her was because they dis-
liked what they considered her conservative views on social ills.

On the tour, disorientation overtook her briefly—she awakened
in her hotel at 3 A.M. looking for her children, who were back in São
Paulo—but she composed herself. She wrote until late morning, when
reporters arrived to interview her. A translator came for her. At the
press conference the questions were friendly, reflecting respect for
her. Audálio Dantas showed up, unannounced, to accompany her.
She was asked, "How can favelas be eradicated?" "What plans do you
have for your life?" "What do you think about the world?" "Is there
racial prejudice in politics?" The Brazilian ambassador sent flowers.
She received applause. Later, in Rosário, she was presented with the
"Order of the Screw," a good-humored award, before three thousand people. A magazine, *Claudia,* paid her to publish a short story,
"The Japanese Man," which she wrote especially for it.

Her answers in the Argentine appendix belie the slurs of Wilson Martins and others years later that Carolina Maria de Jesus was
incapable of intelligent thought. "Illiteracy is the main cause of class
differences," she told the Argentines. "Only if countries provide
basic education for their populations will there be a chance for world
peace. . . . It will take time to solve social problems. . . . Incentives
need to be given to move people to action. . . . Education must not
be an exclusive right for the children of the rich. . . . We need to
organize armies of educators to go into the countryside and into the

forests to teach. . . . The poor require better nutrition. . . . Brazil could be the largest provider of food in Latin America. . . . Industrialists should accept smaller profits to be able to charge lower prices so that the poor can have access to manufactured goods. . . . Land should be made available cheaply so that the poor can leave city slums and return to rural areas, where they can take care of their families." Admirers sent flowers to her hotel room. Carolina rejoiced in the respect that she received. "Argentines are agreeable," she wrote, "they appreciate people [like herself] who work hard, who are honest, who take responsibility." No one attacked her or mocked her, as they did in Brazil. She spoke about world hunger. The Argentine press listened to her courteously. A reporter and photographer took her to "Vila Miseria," a shantytown in Buenos Aires. She remarked that at least its inhabitants had food to eat, and uncontaminated milk. Women were dressed decently, and people had their teeth. Children came up and asked her to put them in her diary so that they "could move into a cinder-block house also." She saw sad things, too. The women complained that water was always in short supply. The women walked dejectedly, never smiling. One woman asked Carolina if poverty was the same elsewhere, and if Jesus would come to Earth to help. Carolina's disorientation continued. "There are moments," she wrote, using the present tense, "that I wanted to run until I fall and die." Another day she wrote that she was "rejuvenating" in Argentina because people were being courteous and friendly to her.

On 27 November 1961 she returned to Brazil for the publication of *Casa de Alvenaria* in Rio de Janeiro. When her Argentine editor visited her a week later in Brazil, she asked him for money to buy a suit for her son João. On 12 December she flew to Montevideo, Uruguay. As in Buenos Aires she was received warmly, put up in the Hotel Lancaster, and asked hard but respectful questions about society and about her opinions and philosophy. She confessed that she never had expected her writing to be published, that she wrote to forget the bitterness of her life. She was struck by how clean the streets were, by the lack of beggars, by the well-dressed and cultured Uruguayans. She was taken to visit a neighborhood of *cantegriles,* a kind of a favela. She noted that much help from charitable groups was available, and that the government was constructing permanent housing, with running water and bathrooms, to replace the shanties. There was a government school in the slum, although many men and youths were without work. She told the slum people who came to see her to plant gardens and raise chickens. When she left the slum she was taken to visit the president of Uruguay in his palace. He embraced her and presided over a luncheon of Brazilian feijoada in her honor. The next day Carolina and the president rode in a motorcade down the streets of the capital to the airport, where they flew to Salto, another Uruguayan city, to dedicate a monument. The archbishop was present, the governor, and the chief of the president's military staff. She spent much of the day with the president. The reception given to Carolina less than a year removed from Canindé favela was stunning, although it was only sparsely reported back home in Brazil.

Her journey continued, back into Argentina, and she took a plane for Santiago, scheduled to cross the Andes to Chile. A motor went out, the plane had to make an unscheduled landing, and she and the other passengers were put in a hotel. Some of them said that they thought she was a rich Ethiopian. In the afternoon she walked the city, stupefied at the elegant dress of the residents, by the gardens, and by the architecture. Children stared at her, unaccustomed to seeing a black person. She continued to walk. Back at the hotel a Brazilian befriended her, and she sat at the piano singing songs she had written. She was awakened at 3 A.M. to go to the airport to resume the flight. After they landed in the Argentine city of Mendoza she prayed to God to protect the airplane, which went on to Peru.

In Mendoza's splendid Parque San Martín, a little girl stopped her and spoke to her, "What country are you from?"

"Brazil."

"Don't they have soap there?"

"Yes."

"Then why don't you wash your skin to make it white?"

". . . My color doesn't come off. I was born this way and this is the way I am."

"We have soap in my house," the girl said. "Let's go to my house . . ."

After lunch, she took a siesta. She dreamed that she lived in a white house, with walls and ceilings of white cotton.

Her visit to Chile commenced on a sour note when she overheard someone at the airport whispering that she was "unmarried and with three children." She pretended not to understand. Dantas had told her that the Chileans had the best manners in Latin America. By now, she was getting homesick. She missed her children. When she was told that the United States was constructing housing for the poor in San Gregorio, outside of Santiago, she made a telling comment on race: "The United States is the great philanthropist for South America. Whites love the United States. But I am black. I have no value for the North Americans. The only black thing they like is petroleum. With petroleum they have no color prejudice."

She became more homesick than ever. She worried that her children might be bothering their neighbors. The Chilean summer was insupportably hot. As she did every day on her tour, she went to another bookstore to autograph copies of the Spanish translation of her first diary. She wrote down that she was getting tired of hearing criticism of her country. "I'm not a politician," she noted. "Books are the only things that interest me."

Her observations became more nuanced. Walking in the street amid the colored Christmas lights, she remarked that Santiago seemed to be a prosperous city but that there were many poor people. People earned 289 *escudos* a month, she learned, but the price of a house and lot was 30,000 *escudos*. She was impressed by the brick buildings and by the lavish parks. Chile, she decided, should build a "great school for the poor children," so that they would not have to beg in the streets. Her diary received an unkind review in the magazine *Ercilla* and in some other journals. People looked at her askance when she ate avocados with lemon and sugar—a common Brazilian custom. High-society women stared at her, she thought, disapprovingly. "Aren't there any unmarried women in Chile?" she wrote. As was her habit, she did not dwell on these disappointments; in response, she wrote in her diary about her inner strength, about being "a woman who does not fear life." "I don't need to marry," she said, especially a stupid man, just to please society. "An educated man, clean, and lovable, perhaps, but God help me if I would have to support a drunk."

A young man invited her to his mother's house for lunch. They went by bus. The house was simple, as was the meal: soup, bread, milk, and salad. She was tired, and the youth let her lie down in his bed. Later, she gave him a copy of her book. That night she went to a literary reception and was interviewed. She talked with the nationalist writer Benjamin Subercaseaux, who, after boasting about Chile— there were no illiterates because the state made schooling obligatory, it was a beautiful country, it was efficient, and so on—told her that she should admire Chile as a tourist but not think of living there. "Our Chileans," he said," "don't like blacks, they don't like Jews, and they don't like Arabs."

She wrote,

> I was shocked because I was born in Brazil and never had heard a white say the word "black" in such a deprecatory tone. Whites in Brazil want to extinguish racial prejudice; the Arabs are prospering, and the Jews like us because they create factories when they give jobs to Brazilians and foreigners living in Brazil. In my country, one's skin color is not important. Only attitudes.

"I felt very cold," she added. She did not eat the dinner that was served. She drank a little wine and became dizzy. Exhausted, she asked to lie down. She could not sleep; she cried "in pain for the blacks, the Arabs, and the Jews." She waited for the dawn so that she could leave Chile. She returned to Buenos Aires and was back in São Paulo the next day. Two weeks later, however, she flew back to Santiago for another four-day book tour. It took so long to get a visa at the Chilean Consulate that she had to pay Cr$4,000 for a taxi so she would not miss her flight. She brought with her a radio to give to the youth and his mother, for having been so warm to her, and smaller presents for others who had befriended her. All throughout her return trip, however, she remembered Subercaseaux's words.

She flew to Concepción, Chile, which she found beautiful although there had been a recent earthquake there, which had destroyed one hundred thousand houses. She appeared at a speakers' forum on international affairs at the university, a prelude to the Punta del Este hemispheric meeting to be held later that month. Professor Gonzalo Rojas spoke first, on social justice, followed by the American Nobel Prize–winning scientist Linus Pauling, who warned about the perils of the nuclear arms race. Carolina noted that she was the only black in attendance. She signed autographs. She was approached by a Chilean professor, Jorge Mendoza Enríquez, who offered to help her. She first had been suspicious (because he followed her around), then intimidated by him ("he was so cultured"). It was "the first time I had even spoken with a professor," she wrote. He invited her that night to have dinner with him and go dancing. They went to two night clubs. They played her song, and she danced with the professor.

She addressed conference participants in a filled lecture hall. These days would be in many ways the high point of her life. She shared the stage with a Russian, Anatoli Zworykin, and Mendoza was with her. Columbia University professor Frank Tannenbaum was to arrive the following day, as well as Mexican novelist Carlos Fuentes and the Cuban writer Alejo Carpentier. A woman friend of Mendoza's drove her around Concepción in the morning. Her speech touched on the migration of poor people to cities, on the burdens of the high cost of living, on the need for education to supplant the effort of nations to destroy one another in war, and on women's responsibility to love and raise their children. The cultural attaché of the Brazilian Embassy translated her talk. Her disappointment with the American professor Frank Tannenbaum's talk led her to declaim in her diary against racism in the United States. "He looked at me with great curiosity," she said. "I realized that he was a racist." She wrote a note and sent it over to him. "As long as racial prejudice exists in the United States, the United States cannot be considered the most cultured country in the world." He replied to her, "I agree with you."[13]

If she was Cinderella, Professor Mendoza was her prince. Again he took her dancing. "I like to be with him," she wrote. "He is cultured and affectionate." "What a spectacular man! How elegant!" "I look at him," she wrote, "and I see no defects. Only good qualities. And I have X-ray eyes!" She signed copies of her book the next day and he visited her again. That night she met the Chilean poet Pablo Neruda at a reception for her. He invited her to his table but she declined, preferring to stay with Mendoza. He accompanied her again, to the Bío Bío River, but this time with his woman friend,

"Professor" Diana. He appeared with Carolina on television. He waited outside the door when Linus Pauling's wife addressed a session "for women only." He told her that he would like to come to Brazil to buy books, and she invited him to stay at her house. He took her dining again, and to hear Neruda. Years later, in 1995, Carolina's daughter Vera observed that Dantas was probably jealous, that he secretly had a crush on her mother.[14] For Carolina, Mendoza was a forbidden dream: a polite, cultured man who respected her, a man who dressed elegantly, "like an actor." When she was not with him she wrote that she missed him. The Spanish edition of Carolina's second diary ends this way: "And my children are already buying gifts for him."

Downward Spiral

Carolina Maria de Jesus' fortunes began to decline as soon as she returned to São Paulo from her second trip to Chile. This would be the last of her publicity tours. The flood of requests for interviews and radio and television appearances stopped, although journalists continued to consider her fair game and dropped in, if now sporadically, at any time. Her royalties diminished abruptly. Although *Quarto de Despejo* became an international sensation, translated into more than a dozen languages and sold around the world, her publisher never anticipated the amount of success the translated diary would have. As already noted, the press sold the rights to foreign literary agents who then received the bulk of the royalties. Carolina would receive some payments from the United States, Holland, and France, but these were not very substantial. She never received a single royalty check from any other country. There were a few payments for movie rights but, except for a documentary made in Germany and another by TV Globo in Brazil, little came of the projects to film her life story. Publishers of her last two books issued while she was alive (*Pedaços da Fome* [Pieces of hunger] and *Provérbios* [Proverbs]) made her subsidize them heavily, and they were commercial failures.[15] Her beloved poems went unpublished and her career as a songwriter and recording artist went nowhere.

Members of the elite, some of whom invited her to dine, or who honored her (at the University of São Paulo Law School, for example, and at the city's Academy of Letters), quickly tired of her feisty personality and her unschooled manners. The left rejected her from the start because she was considered insufficiently revolutionary, selfish—concerned only about herself and her children—and a believer in the work ethic, which they considered a device to keep the population docile. Intellectuals dismissed her because her writing contained errors, because she dressed badly, and because she voiced opinions that they considered childish or naive. Conservative literary critics not only refused to see any value in either her prose narratives, autobiographical writing, or fiction, but called her a "literary fake" because they could not believe that someone like Carolina was capable of even writing a diary. One newspaper editor, shown one of her poems before she became famous, yelled at her that she should write on toilet paper.

Her troubles with her neighbors increased. People continually showed up at her door, asking for financial help. She may have spent much of her royalties on helping people. Dantas and others claim that she may have been swindled or deceived by men who pretended to like her. Many of her expenses were for luxuries that others take for granted but for her were extraordinary: for example, she hired a private tutor so that one of her children could catch up in school and made extensive repairs to her house. In spite of all of this, Carolina could not adjust to middle-class life, and she decided to break her ties with the people who had helped her when she became famous. She used all of the rest of her financial assets to buy a piece of land in Parelheiros, a then-rural zone on the periphery of São Paulo that soon would become polluted as the city's industrial belt expanded outward. In Parelheiros she lived in a house she and her children largely constructed themselves. After her move, for a time they were so poor that she had to ride buses to the city with her burlap sack to hunt for paper, metal, and discarded food. The press ran stories on this—Carolina as a scavenger was still good copy.

When she died in 1977 she was a recluse. As a nontraditional author whose untutored writing lacked polish and who spoke about matters considered banal by most intellectuals, Carolina's work has been excluded from the Brazilian literary canon. Irving Stern's four-hundred-page *Dictionary of Brazilian Literature* (New York: Greenwood,

1988) devotes only two lines to her. She has never been included in a standard anthology. Her best-seller, *Quarto de Despejo*, remained out of print for years. Only a single critic, Marisa Lajolo of UNICAMP, publicly acknowledged, in 1995, in the preface to the Brazilian edition of Carolina's biography, that Carolina's story contained valuable lessons. Carolina died, she noted, in 1977, the same year that José Louzeiro published a novel about the evils of street life. Louzeiro's book inspired the Argentine film maker Hector Babenco to make his stunning Brazilian-produced film, *Pixote, the Law of the Weakest* (1981), whose principal child actor, Fernando Ramos da Silva, was slain by the São Paulo police in 1987. The blight of urban poverty depicted by Carolina Maria de Jesus in 1960 had not only continued in Brazil but it had become much more pervasive and violent.[16]

Carolina never understood the symbolism of her ascent from misery. Fame for her was a path to having food to eat every day and a house in which to live. She never saw herself as a role model, or as a crusader. This is one of the main reasons that Brazilian intellectuals rejected her: they saw her as self-centered, looking out only for herself and her children. Yet how could it have been otherwise? Few really listened to her or took her observations seriously. Her resolve never to marry because of men's treatment of her and out of fear of losing her independence was a courageous feminist act, but female Brazilian intellectuals never recognized this. Women reporters who interviewed her chastened Carolina for wearing ill-matched clothing and for not knowing how to walk in high-heeled shoes.

Even after her initial success, only a few Brazilians saw her as something more than a curiosity. It is also likely that some resented the fact that the fathers of her children had all been white men, a prejudice expressed more openly in the Brazil of the 1950s and 1960s than later. Even the marriage during the early 1960s of the great soccer star Pelé to a blonde white woman was severely criticized, and Pelé's wedding was held in Germany, not in the country that revered him for his athleticism.

Only a small number of Brazilians saw in Carolina's published diary entries ammunition for advocating social reform, and these voices were silenced during the nearly twenty years of dictatorship imposed by the military coup of 31 March 1964. The media frenzy that briefly enveloped her in Brazil came from her curiosity value because social norms could not accept a black favelada as an author. Only a small group of São Paulo black intellectuals; the manager of the Pinheiros Sport Club, who held a dance in her honor; and a few others embraced her unconditionally. Although the harsh light of her first diary led city officials to tear down Canindé favela, the number of favela dwellers in São Paulo rose precipitously over the years. Today they live under conditions much worse than those suffered by Carolina, with considerably higher rates of drug use, overcrowding, crime, and disease.

I'm Going to Have a Little House is above all a straightforward autobiography. Carolina's diary entries allowed her to assign meaning to the experiences of her life. Her courage in persisting in her writing year after year even as a marginalized social castoff—as a black, a woman, and a rural-born migrant with two years of school and no skills or training—is remarkable. She is acutely aware of Brazil's lack of racial democracy yet she is comfortable with her blackness. She writes, years before it became fashionable, that "natural is beautiful" when a child suggests she straighten her kinky hair. She is aware of her dual role as author and protagonist, a circumstance that places her diaries of marginality well within the boundaries of the contemporary self-conscious narrative. The reader of *I'm Going to Have a Little House* comes away with the impression that Carolina is always fully aware that the sudden change in her status, from garbage-dump scavenger to published author, does not alter the fundamental outrage of her alienated condition.[17]

notes

Diary

1. Carolina usually does not capitalize "Sr." (Senhor, or Mister), although in Portuguese, as in English, this title is capitalized. She does capitalize "Dr.," however. Sometimes she refers to the same person as Sr. on some occasions and Dr. on others.
2. "Cr$" is the symbol for the Brazilian currency unit, the cruzeiro.
3. Caryl Chessman was a confessed rapist and serial killer whose execution in the United States created a storm of protest among humanitarians and intellectuals worldwide against capital punishment.
4. Here in the diary, for the first time, Carolina refers to Dantas as "the reporter," a change from her previous use of his first name. From this point on she mixes the two usages, but ultimately calls him only "the reporter."
5. She writes "spiquer," a Brazilian adaptation of the English word "speaker."
6. Actually, a *bonde*, or electric bus. The word *bonde* came from the English word "bonds," which were floated to permit Brazilian cities to acquire electrified urban transport.
7. Carolina frequently gives the address of places she visits. In part this is a function of her literal-mindedness in her diary writing, but, given that her citations of addresses increase as the publication of her book nears, it also reflects her astonishment at her newly found fortune in being able to go to such prestigious places.
8. Raw sugar-cane alcohol, the drink of lower-class men and women.
9. The drawing depicts a shocking incident recorded in Carolina's first published diary, *Quarto de Despejo*, in which a beggar was given a package of dead rats.
10. *Dona* is the feminine form of the Spanish-Portuguese honorific *Dom* [*Don*], used as a term of respect for married women. Audálio Dantas's use of the word for Carolina is ironic because she was unmarried.

11. He was probably one of the people to whom she sold paper and bottles. Later in the diary she uses the spelling *Scharauffer.*
12. The word *brincos* [earrings] can also mean "toys" in old usage.
13. The cabbie uses "credo," a word used by those born in Minas Gerais that is akin to saying "Jesus."
14. In *Casa de Alvenaria,* Dantas provides a footnote identifying Correia Leite as an "element connected with the black cultural movement in São Paulo."
15. In *Casa de Alvenaria,* Dantas identifies "Delegado" in a footnote as a "very popular Negro, well known in colored associations."
16. *O Cruzeiro* was one of Brazil's two leading national illustrated news magazines, akin to *Life* in the United States. This was a major achievement for Carolina.
17. Lacking proper documentation because she was indigent and illegitimate, Carolina would not have been permitted to transact banking business without her sponsor being present.
18. Leila was a prostitute who had stabbed Carolina several times when Leila had come after João, whom the prostitute had accused of taunting her. Carolina was in the hospital for weeks.
19. Carolina is making a reference to a metaphor she employed in *Quarto de Despejo.* In that work she identified the room in a house where trash is stored as the abode of the poor; those who were more fortunate and prosperous lived in the "living room."
20. Carolina uses the word *bares,* "bar," indicating that she ate at working-class cafés where simple meals, usually rice, beans, and a little meat, were served as well as beer and *pinga* to drink.
21. At this point in *Casa de Alvenaria,* Dantas inserts a footnote: "Many people showed up after the publicity engendered by the book to protect the 'poor favela dweller'" (his quotation marks).
22. Actually, Valdir was law school dean.
23. Carolina's paragraph says only this. Apparently someone asked a question linking race to favela poverty.
24. São Paulo buses from working-class neighborhoods were expensive (a round trip cost as much as a third of a worker's daily wage), crowded, dirty, and uncomfortable.
25. Augusta Street was São Paulo's most elegant shopping district in the late 1950s and early 1960s.
26. The Matarazzo clan was one of the wealthiest in São Paulo. Eduardo was from the Suplicy branch of the family, which, more than the others, devoted themselves to progressive social causes. He went on to be a

senator for the Labor Party (PT) and ran for mayor. He also taught law at the University of São Paulo.

27. An *algueire* is a measure of land akin to an acre.

28. *Manchete* was Brazil's second most important weekly magazine after *O Cruzeiro.*

29. Mãe Preta (literally, "black nanny") was an annual holiday in honor of nursemaids and other servants, almost all of whom were black.

30. This was the samba composition Carolina had written and later recorded commercially at her own expense.

31. The U.S. comic strip character.

32. Sr. Monteiro was one of the fifteen people living in the house that, according to the contract, was to be given to Carolina on 20 December.

33. A poor neighborhood on the fringes of São Paulo.

34. She uses the formal address for a fellow writer, not because they are at the same social level.

35. She actually calls him a *moreno*, a polite term referring to a light-complexioned black, although Carolina does this for all blacks she likes, even if they are technically not *morenos* because they have darker skin.

36. Dona Edy Lima was the scriptwriter of *Quarto de Despejo*'s theatrical adaptation.

37. This is an example of Carolina's distrust of people who are trying to help her. When the teacher suggests that João have a tutor, Carolina emphasizes the fact that the tutor would be the teacher's friend, implying a kind of payoff.

38. TV Cultura, the state-run educational television station.

39. Carolina has been invited to participate in a program in which housewives would converse with the wives of candidates for mayor of São Paulo.

40. Actually, Dantas received 5 percent and Carolina 10 percent of the royalties from the Brazilian sales of her two published diaries.

41. Coutinho was a soccer player and teammate of Pelé.

42. This was a *very* high salary for maids in Brazil at the time.

43. Because of the low wages paid for skilled labor, it was always less costly to have clothing made to order than to buy ready-made clothing, sold only in boutiques. There were few department stores in the 1950s and early 1960s, and their prices for clothing were high.

44. Apparently, Carolina still cannot sign her own checks or withdraw money from her own bank account.

45. Zélia Gatai, also a writer and author of a book of memoirs about her life in São Paulo at the beginning of the century.
46. Carolina always felt herself a rival to Jorge Amado, at that time Brazil's most prolific novelist. The parenthetical ellipses, of course, indicate editing by Dantas. Did he remove some unkind comment?
47. This is a pun, whether intentional or not. Another meaning of the term *mãe preta* refers to a ritualistic maternal figure in the Afro-Brazilian spiritist cults.
48. Carolina's final diary comment is ambiguous. Did she go to lunch and then take a taxi home? Or was she so weary that she declined Dona Filomena's invitation?

Afterword

1. Quotes taken from advertisements for diary. *O Estado de São Paulo* clipping file.
2. Mario Trejo, preface to Carolina Maria de Jesus, *La Favela* (Havana: Casa de las Americas, 1965), n.p.
3. Audálio Dantas, preface to *Casa de Alvenaria: Diário de uma ex-favelada* (Rio de Janeiro: Editora Paulo de Azevedo Ltda., 1961), n.p. Italics in original.
4. Ann Frost, translator's note to Maria Odila Silva Dias, *Power and Everyday Life: The Lives of Working Women in Nineteenth-Century Brazil* (London: Polity Press, 1995), xii.
5. This sentiment still held fast a generation after Carolina's diary was published. See the statement "Sofrer e Calar" by "Flávia," in Frances O'Gorman, *Morro, Mulher* (São Paulo: Edições Paulinas, 1984), 21.
6. Tad Szulc, review of *Child of the Dark, New York Times Book Review,* 23 September 1962.
7. Dantas, preface.
8. Wilson Martins, "Mistificação literária," *Jornal do Brasil* (Rio de Janeiro), 23 October 1993. Dantas replied in *Jornal do Brasil,* 11 December 1993, n.p. (clipping sent to author by Wilson Martins).
9. Some of these observations are taken from Melvin S. Arrington Jr., "From the Garbage Dump to the Brick House: The Diaries of Carolina Maria de Jesus," *South Eastern Latin Americanist* 36 (spring 1993): 1–12.
10. Readers not familiar with Brazilian racial terminology should note that, as in the United States, the word "white" connotes a person of Caucasian ancestry, whereas in Brazil racial identity historically has been based as much on economic status as on racial lineage. "Black" in the United States means anyone with known African (or Negroid)

ancestry, including light-skinned persons of mixed-race background. In Brazil, "black" is used only for persons of very dark skin. Other terms are used to describe persons of intermediary mixtures, including *mulatos* (persons with mostly African and Caucasian background) and *caboclos* (persons of mixed American Indian, African, and Caucasian origin).

11. Carolina Maria de Jesus, "Apéndice: Diario de viaje (Argentina-Uruguay-Chile)" *Casa de ladrillos,* (Buenos Aires: Editorial Abraxas, 1963), 128–91.

12. Not everyone in Argentina held Carolina in adulation. I was an undergraduate exchange student in Mendoza when she arrived for her publicity tour in 1961. I had been curious about what I read in the newspaper about her, but the family with whom I was living scoffed at her; one university professor called her a "Brazilian monkey." I was not able to see her during the few days she was in Argentina.

13. She attended one of Tannenbaum's two talks but believed that they went badly: he refused to answer the questions put to him, and he sounded confused, she said. She called the Columbia University professor "the black sheep" of the conference. Tannenbaum, the founder of the Columbia University Seminars and a personal friend of democratic Latin American presidents, had a reputation throughout his career as a humane man who advocated close hemispheric relations and who was considered in the United States to be an outspoken liberal.

14. When Dantas was shown a photograph of Carolina with Mendoza and her children, he launched into a tirade, saying that Mendoza "could never have been a university professor" and that he was surely only after Carolina's royalties." Vera Eunice de Jesus Lima, personal communication, São Paulo, 16 April 1995.

15. The story of Carolina's royalties and her other published books is told in Robert M. Levine and José Carlos Sebe Bom Meihy, *The Life and Death of Carolina Maria de Jesus* (Albuquerque: University of New Mexico Press, 1995).

16. Marisa Lajolo, preface to Robert M. Levine and José Carlos Sebe Bom Meihy, *Cinderela Negra: A Saga de Carolina Maria de Jesus* (Rio de Janeiro: Editora UFRJ, 1995), i–ii. UNICAMP is the State University of São Paulo at Campinas.

17. See Arrington, "From the Garbage Dump to the Brick House," 8.

In the Engendering Latin America series

Volume 1
Sex and Danger in Buenos Aires:
Prostitution, Family, and Nation in Argentina
DONNA J. GUY

Volume 2
Between Civilization and Barbarism:
Women, Nation, and Literary Culture
in Modern Argentina
FRANCINE MASIELLO

Volume 3
Women, Feminism, and Social Change
in Argentina, Chile, and Uruguay, 1890–1940
ASUNCIÓN LAVRIN

Volume 4
I'm Going to Have a Little House:
The Second Diary of Carolina Maria de Jesus
CAROLINA MARIA DE JESUS
Translated by Melvin S. Arrington Jr.
and Robert M. Levine